PAREN
Happy
High Achievers

Marjorie DelBello, Ed.D.

Parents of Happy High Achievers
By Marjorie DelBello, Ed.D.

Copyright February 2013

Printed in U.S.A.

ISBN: 978-1482544244

Cover design and inside layout by Parry Design Studio, Inc.

DEDICATION

For Jim, who's always there; And for my children: Catherine and Jimmy, And my grandchildren: Sydney and James Rocco who have provided me with my own personal learning lab.

ACKNOWLEDGEMENTS

No one writes a book like this alone. I'm indebted to so many for its completion.

First, to the "Wonder Parents," and all the parents and families I have known through the years, I extend my deepest thanks. Your ideas, opinions, suggestions and generous sharing having inspired me and prodded me to learn more. It's been an honor and joy to work with you.

To my own family, I can never thank you enough for your patience and loving support.

Appreciation also goes to my colleagues, Beverly Smith, Barbara Shaw, Pat Dunn, Jeff Davis, Dr. Anthony V. Costello, Dr. Cynthia Strauss, and Dr. Jane Bowers, for their ongoing collaboration and assistance in analyzing and identifying many of the complex dynamics that flowed beneath the surface of many case studies. Thanks, too, to the entire staff and administration of the Garnet Valley and Rose Tree Media School Districts. Countless were the hours spent together in multi-disciplinary meetings.

To my special friends that have supported and encouraged me through the years—Sanka Coyle, the Sullivan cheerleaders: Maureen, Sharon, and Eileen; also Barbara Jones, Barbara Tarr, I am so grateful. To Lois McNicol and Carol Kennedy who took a special interest in the project and lent technical assistance, I extend many thanks.

Last, but certainly not least, I thank literary and design consultants Bill Quain, Jack and Elizabeth Parry, and my editor, Jeannine Norris for their patience, attention to detail, and remarkable skill. Without their help and encouragement, this book would never have happened.

PREFACE

These are exciting times! Times of interesting new knowledge! Lots of it! More has been discovered in the past few decades than in all the previous centuries combined. Some are even calling ours the age of a Great Knowledge Revolution.

Take neuroscience for example. Scientists have introduced us to "plasticity," and "neuroplasticity"—qualities of our bodies and brains that reveal that we are more amorphous, changeable and adaptable than we ever dreamed possible. By applying effort, drive, patience, and persistence, we now have proof that we can become smarter, stronger, faster and more adept at almost anything we desire. Like 'Plastic Man' or 'Gumby' we can stretch ourselves to meet new and lofty goals and kids can do the same. Science tells us that no one knows their limits until they try. It's an optimistic and motivating message for our age.

Remember that expression: "Biology is Destiny"? Gone. Kicked off its high horse! And do you recall Gregor Mendel—the monk with all the neat little rows of pea pods related to heredity they taught us in biology class? Even his venerable work had to be given a second look, and overhauled a bit. (Turns out that two blue-eyed parents can have a brown-eyed child.) How about that? Yes, times have changed—particularly how science views our potential.

Genes, of course, are still enormously important. They are just no longer viewed as the be-all and end-all. It's the interaction of genes and the environment that matters most, and humans can control much of that. Our experiences and environment turn genes on or off. When we act, we flip internal switches and turn knobs that allow genes to change. This can expand and sculpt our minds and bodies, and do the same for our children. Every day in every way, through our actions and choices, we are determining what kind of person we and our children will be tomorrow.

And what's most exciting is that we've been given proof. (It's no longer just a motivational speaker's opinion that we can become all we want to be.) With new technologies, science has provided us with solid observable measurable evidence that this is, indeed, fact.

But many have yet to credit this good news. Even savvy educated parents who brag about the dramatic results they've seen through their own physical workouts don't always make the connection to parenting power. Focused recurrent efforts over time can re-sculpt their kids—if only more would use them. But too often they're held back by outdated myths.

"You can't tell me all those smart kids weren't just born that way," you hear some balk. "It's all in the genes. Heredity rules. There's very little that parents can do to change the basic package, so why bother?" Or "Our family lacks math genes" or "music genes;" or "We all have fat genes." Such mindsets limit one's horizons.

Another common misconception is that if a particular child does not show early signs of precocity, he never will. This, too, is untrue. It's very limiting and contrary to what we now know.

Still, parents do wonder about potential and commonly look for answers. Frequently, we hear questions such as these:

"Are talents in the genes?"

"What part does the environment play?"

"How can I best draw out my child's gifts and give him an extra boost?"

"Is it worth the extra effort, or will nature have its way?"

"Are there subtleties and nuances I should know about?"

"And, by the way: Who are the parents of these brainiacs in our midst?"

"What do they know that I do not?"

Parents don't always go to the internet or the media for answers, but they continue to raise the questions. I know because as long as I've been in education (forty-plus years), I've heard them and still do today.

But there are some exceptions! I've noticed that there are, and always seem to have been, a small core of parents who don't seem puzzled by these issues. They just move ahead with confidence and their children shine as bright as stars—right to the top. They ask few questions. They don't wait for neuroscience to declare our "plasticity," or other directional signals. They just move ahead. A few such parents have slow starters, but that doesn't matter to them. They persevere unfazed, and sure enough, those children, too, reach the pinnacle. I dubbed these parents "HAPs"—a nickname for "Highest Achievers' Parents." They are the parents of the happy top achievers—the future valedictorians, salutatorians, and other coveted award winners, who excel in every way.

The HAPs always fascinated me. From the get-go, they seemed to know so much. I began studying them intensively—observing, listening, engaging them when I could and taking notes. I cross-referenced their beliefs and strategies with the research. As an educator and teacher of the gifted, my interest in "talent development" came naturally and only grew as I climbed the career ladder, and encountered more and more HAPs, and more and more questions from parents.

(As to be expected, I discovered a few hyper-competitive types among the HAP population, but I screened them out. They did not seem authentic role models and I noticed they often got push-back from their children. So I decided to focus on the parents of the HAPPY high achievers.)

Luckily, there were many such HAPs through the years. And boy were they a chatty bunch! They held strong opinions and loved to talk about all things related to children and education.

This suited me fine, for I also did. Through their actions, as well as words, they told stories. If there was a question about the school needing a library expansion, I noticed they'd be on the school board's doorsteps immediately. The library would soon appear. If they caught wind of a possible new testing protocol or textbook adoption they were "on it"—asking all the right questions, and collaborating to get the job done right. To say they were generally active and involved would be an understatement.

HAPs shared their ideas generously and dazzled me with their wisdom, insight and common sense, and I continued to study every aspect of their parenting styles and personal philosophies. I made particular note of any and all recommendations relating to talent development.

My job helped, too, of course. As part of my duties, I was required to observe and work with pupils and families, review student records (including parent input forms), attend conferences, chair multi-disciplinary meetings, and collaborate with parents, teachers and psychologists on an array of issues. We analyzed, triangulated and brainstormed creative methods of meeting students' needs. We engaged in "side bars" after meetings, chit chats at banquets, small talk in the bleachers at games, banter on field trips, and exchanges as we worked side by side at the May Fair, or Winterfest. I picked up many, many pointers.

I also lived near my work, which gave me other ample opportunities to just "hang out" with HAPs. I observed families at work and at play, and zeroed in on many nuances of effective parenting. (In retrospect, it's amazing what I learned at neighborhood parties and even by the frozen food case in the local supermarket.) Brrr. Cold. But informative. And all duly noted.

(Of course, *all* parents educated me. It would be foolish to say that HAPs cornered the market on wisdom, but it seemed that HAPs were particularly informative.)

The years flew. The data mounted—rich and relevant. I stayed abreast of the literature, exploring areas specifically related to parental insights and recommendations. (Because much of my information was anecdotal, I felt compelled to study the research from controlled studies on related topics to provide balance and perspective.)

Upon retirement, I sifted through my mountains of data and searched for meaning. In time, Voila! Patterns emerged; commonalities congealed; and the project took shape. Three core beliefs and forty-five recommended strategies rose to the top. There were many more of course, but these stood out for a number of reasons:

1. They were recurrent and were shared with the greatest degree of intensity and frequency through the years by the HAPs.

2. They were consistent with current research, and

3. They reportedly made the child rearing years productive and joyful ones for the HAPs and for their children.

These beliefs and strategies form the basis of this book.

The work is divided into two major parts: Part One presents an overview of the three core beliefs that HAPs believed drove their best practices. Part Two is a collection of the HAP's "greatest hits"—forty five strategies and interventions that were most highly recommended.

The tome admittedly covers a lot of territory. There is much information and many lists—perhaps too many to be digested at one time. (Remember, this was forty plus years of input.) So the reader may initially want to familiarize himself with an overview and then return to specific sections as they command his interests, as we do with a handbook.

Looking back, I find it interesting that much of what is now shared by those in the cognitive and neurosciences, was long intuited by HAPs. Other HAPs came to it through their cultural backgrounds or parental modeling. But what does it matter? With some basic information, anyone can learn to raise a happy high achiever today. Hopefully, this book will help.

TABLE OF CONTENTS

Part 1:

Three Key Belief Systems

◆　◆　◆

BELIEF SYSTEMS:

Beliefs drive actions. Research confirms this. Beliefs act like software running in the back of our minds to help us refine our goals and direct our decisions. Scholars, Carol Dweck and Albert Bandura of Stanford University, have shown that one's <u>beliefs</u> can affect how far one goes in life. People who *believe* they can accomplish what they set out to do, perform better than those who don't. (If you *believe* you will perform well, then you probably will. If you *believe* you won't, you probably won't.) In fact it's been shown that what you believe is more important than how objectively talented you are.

Almost every successful and confident parent I have known held the following beliefs about parenting and were convinced that they were linked to their child's high performance:

Belief Number One:

Almost every child has unlimited potential. Parents can do much to draw that out.

Belief Number Two:

Effort and hard work are at the root of achievement, and hard work can offset lesser ability.

Belief Number Three:

Balance and an emphasis on the "Whole Child" (the physical, affective, cognitive, and transcendent domains) are essential to overall success.

Chapter 1:
Belief Number One: Potential

Almost every child has unlimited potential—at least in some areas—and parents can draw that out.

Today, many people believe in human potential, but "back in the day,"—in the mid- 1960's, when I first started teaching, this belief was not widespread. You would commonly overhear things such as: "Oh, go on. You can't tell me those smart kids aren't just born that way. I know better. They won some lottery at conception. It's all in their genes. You either have it or you don't… You win or you lose. And you can't change that."

But there was always a small core of parents who disagreed. Despite the fact that there was no evidence of potential either way, they trusted their own instincts. Condoleeza Rice's parents were a good example. Condi said that "despite the fact that my parents couldn't take me down to Woolworth's for a hamburger, they made me feel that I could become President of the United States." And of course, she came close—she was appointed Secretary of State. Hats off to the Rice's and all the other parents who telegraph such confident messages to their children, despite circumstances.

But the Rice's were actually the exception. In Condi's day, most parents were more laid back, and the majority deferred to the genes.

"Show me the proof that it's otherwise," one angry father shouted on his way in to a meeting when another parent tried to convince him that it was the parents' job to take the reins.

"It's up to us to inspire and draw out our children's talents… Genes are important, but more so is the environment," she had said.

"Prove it. "

"I have no proof. I just know it to be so. Call it instinct. Call it spidey vibes. Call it what you want… But I believe they're all programmed to be phenomenal—at least in certain areas, and it's up to the parents to inspire and draw out all that potential. Anyone can do it…"

"How?"

"With lots of small actions that add up over time."

That parent in the "nurture camp,"—on the side of environment— was a HAP, and her passion and belief were typical of HAPs back then—just as they are today. In fact, in time I would discover it was one of the HAPs major hallmarks and most deep-seated convictions. They talked about it frequently.

I began to notice a pattern: The children of parents who spoke strongly and with deep assurance regarding potential performed the best in school (and often all around.) Meanwhile, parents who were convinced that the *genes* dictated success tended to hesitate a lot. Typically, they took a total hands-off policy. Their children often did not do as well academically, whereas the HAPs' children exhibited confidence and usually rose to their parents' expectations.

Let me share a little history lesson as background:

When I began to teach in the 1960's, pediatricians and teachers clearly exuded absolute authority over matters pertaining to nature or nurture. And mostly they favored nature—the genes. They implied that babies and children were akin to "automatons," little programmed creatures who would flourish in due course if you just left them alone. In fact, they were instructed to leave them

4

alone. "They're like little flowers that will blossom when they are ready. It's best not to interfere." Both teachers and pediatricians were on the same page. "Nature is in charge, so let Mother Nature just do her job."

"If you encourage them to walk before they're ready, they may be bowlegged; if you try to teach them to read too early, they'll turn off to language. So, whatever you do, don't let them go ahead in the basal reader. We'll direct the pace at school. You'll do more harm than good." Mostly, parents complied. It seemed as though the pediatricians, psychologists and teachers were in cahoots.

"Biology is Destiny" rang out from every Biology I classroom in the land back then (and ditzy sophomores, longing to justify their raging hormones, gleefully embraced it.) And DNA, newly discovered with its own PR machine of glitz and power, was frequently used to impress one. When DNA was mentioned, you were expected to fall back in awe, acclaim its primacy, and accede to it omniscient powers. It went without saying that if you had good DNA, then you were intelligent. If not, well… too bad. You were out of luck, and probably doomed to an inferior life. DNA was what counted.

Feeling relatively powerless, most parents took solace knowing that they were "good enough," if they "provided a level of care that protected the child from harm" according to psychologists. They accepted that their main role was to be patient and wait for the genes to dictate the program.

But the parents that balked—mostly HAPs—secretly admitted to responding to baby's every need. They would sing and talk to the fetus in utero, aggressively enrich him from the moment he was born, and study him from morning to night. They came to know every nuance and subtlety of the child's temperament and interests, strengths and needs, and they delighted in learning these as they unfurled. They responded, reciprocated and mimicked his actions. Some even had the temerity to move ahead in the basal reader when the child reached school age. Unimaginable!

Nature Versus Nurture

Then in the late '60's and early '70's, things began to change. Blind faith in the system faded; compliance became passé; and everyone questioned everything. War broke out in Vietnam, civil rights and environmental policies came under scrutiny, and many thought it was time for "Fifty Two Pick-up"—a complete overhaul of society. No concept was beyond reproach, and the nature/nurture controversy took on new fervor:

"It's nature." "No, nurture."

"Talent is innate." "No, it's developed."

"Genes matter most." "No, it's the environment."

"Inborn." "No, effort."

"Hard wired." "No, hard work"

"Heritable." "No, learned."

The fur frequently flew at meetings. Science did little to quell the disturbance or resolve the controversy, because there was no definitive proof either way at the time.

I remember posting a notice of a parent meeting in our district's middle school library—one of many back then to discuss the issue, and wondering why I bothered. Unrest was in the air, again, and as we headed into the room, a full-scale rumble seemed imminent.

"I resent your stand," a genetic-determinist father spat to a HAP parent as soon as he heard a remark about the primacy of the environment. "You can't tell me your little brainiacs weren't just born that way. It's all in their genes. You know it and I know it. Your human potential stuff is all crap. And don't try to give me a guilt trip because you think maybe I'm not doing enough with my kids."

The calm mother tried to defuse things: "Don't you think anyone can become smart? Being smart is just an accumulation of lots of small things—including some that start before birth—accompanied by hard work. Any parent can help with this. We influence the genes. Yes. It requires some extra effort, but I think it's good news. Hopeful. It's no reason to get your nose out of joint."

"Sure. Easy for you to say. Prove it."

Of course the parent couldn't. There was no hard evidence either way, so HAPs just went on doing what they were doing, and the nature/nurture controversy continued to divide parents and keep some wobbly in their views.

Science Has a Breakthrough: Expertise Studies.

Then in 1980 something happened that slowed down the blind faith of the "nature" camp—or genetic determinists, as they were known. It encouraged the HAPs and others who believed environmental forces could help mold genes. Psychologists K.A. Ericsson and W.G. Chase took a man of very average ability and taught him to perform incredible feats of memory. (For example, while most of us can only remember a sequence of seven or eight digits, this man was taught to instantly recall a fantastic 55 digits at a time.)

This astounded many and raised an important question: If this very average student could be taught to be exceptional, was it possible that anyone could be taught anything under the right circumstances? Could "average" genes be coaxed to exceed average expectations?

The event set off a rash of "expertise studies" that lasted over twenty years, probing every possible niche for evidence that environmental influences could interact and affect genes.

Scientists pulled apart learning. They studied all kinds of people from diffcrent walks of life. The questions they asked mirrored what many parents had struggled with:

What impact does practice have on achievement?

What part does persistence play?

What is memory and how does it work?

What is the true nature of cognition?

What about mentors? How do they affect the learning process?

How important are creativity and innovation?

What part does muscle response play?

What separates mediocrity from excellence?

What is "genius?" Can anyone become one?

Is there such a thing as "born genius?"

What role do rigor and training play?

Thousands of such studies took place. One notable one was led by Dr. Benjamin Bloom at the University of Chicago, whose team scoured the country for 120 super-achievers—people named by their peers as the "top of the top"—the "best of the best" in their fields (mathematics, chess, neuroscience, tennis, music, and sculpture). Then the researchers interviewed the subjects and their parents, probing their backgrounds, hoping to learn as much as possible about the roots and trajectories of their demonstrated greatness. What happened in their youth that determined the course of their careers? Surprisingly, many stated the "greats" were not especially talented in their early years, but gradually "fell in love with their field" and this, then, drove them on. Most had expert mentors and spiraling goals once their sights were set, and mostly they all spoke of a commitment to lots of practice and grit and grunt work. What was the parents' role? The parents provided ongoing attention, interest, encouragement and enthusiasm. Yes, they were very involved with the child and their dreams in the early years, and helped the "romance" of the field along. Once the basics were grounded, and a good tutor was in place, the parents pulled back, and watched from the periphery.

The expertise studies also involved a re-examination of the trajectories of some great geniuses, including Wolfgang Amadeus Mozart—the poster boy of all child geniuses—and one who most assume was a "born genius." Dr. Robert Weisberg of Temple University, and others who studied Mozart's life in depth, saw it differently, though. While it's true that Mozart grew into the title of "musical genius," he was not born that way. His early work, they discovered, was noteworthy, but actually no better than some works of his peers. In fact, his early work was described as a hodge-podge of pieces, mostly taken from other composers. Working for Mozart was the fact that his entire family was highly musical, and even in utero, the developing baby was bathed in music, presumably, feeding his natural proclivity. Later, as an infant and toddler, Mozart continued to be exposed to extreme amounts of great music, and high-caliber instruction. It was here, experts surmised, that a gradual accretion of environmental influences built up. Little by little, he grew into his gifts. But it took years for that to happen—many years of extremely hard work—along with coaching, perseverance, acquired love of the music and self-discipline. At one point, Mozart wrote to his father: "People make a great mistake who think that my art has come easily to me. Nobody has devoted so much time and thought to composition as I." Of course, we know that Mozart eventually ascended to the pinnacle of his field, but only then did he deserve the reputation of a true musical "genius."

Similar studies were done to analyze other accomplished figures, with similar findings. Beethoven, for example, was found to have rewritten some of his compositions as many as sixty or seventy times before he was satisfied.

Yes, it is true that some individuals *are* born with proclivities that hearken promise of great talent. We usually call them prodigies. Every age has them, and often much ado is made of their abilities when they appear on the scene. But studies show that few prodigies go on to become top adult achievers. Most fizzle out. Unlike Bloom's "greats" and Mozart (whose father saw to it that the young Wolfgang never let up) the typical child prodigy does not put forth the sustained kind of effort needed to rise to the top. Very few prodigies ever reach the pinnacle of their fields. (Conversely, many slow starters do, and again, that is attributed to enormous sustained effort and skillful mentoring.) All through the 1980's and 1990's evidence of latent potential mounted, drawn forth by the effects of such effort. Those were days of heated discussion, much research, and controversy.

In the end, after years of such studies, the collective results of numerous researchers came in. They were conclusive: **TALENT WAS NOT THE <u>CAUSE</u>, BUT THE <u>RESULT</u> OF SOMETHING.** This was virtually a new concept, and very big. Many studies drew the same conclusion. Finally, science could offer proof that human potential is not endowed, but earned over time. Talent and achievement were not inborn, but earned. The experts also concluded that it no longer made sense to use the term "born genius." It was now viewed as misleading and out-moded. "Biology is destiny" was finally kicked off its high horse.

A new view replaced it, and a new, more hopeful slogan, emerged. This one aligned to what HAPs espoused all along:

"<u>Nature loads the gun. But nurture pulls the trigger.</u>"

Yes, genes are important, but without environmental stimulation, many genes will never be expressed. It is the interaction of the genes and the environment that counts the most, and those are irrevocably intermeshed throughout life.

The rise of the neurosciences and the development of new technologies played an instrumental role in this discovery. It was helpful that previous skeptics, with the help of new technologies, such as: Pet scans, CT scans and fMRI's could see clear evidence of the impact of the environment on physiology.

Examples include:

Brains before and after smoking

Brains before and after drugs

Brains before and after exercise

Brains before and after meditation

Brains before and after memorizing, switching tasks, and paying acute attention to a piece of work.

It became harder to deny the human role in our intelligence. Evidence of what environmental factors could elicit was clear and human potential was given a boost.

Beyond Expertise Studies: Discovering Our Plastic Selves.

Research in all the sciences took an enormous leap in the decades toward the end of the twentieth century. Thousands and thousands of experiments in various fields—all involving the manipulation of environmental factors—were conducted. Researchers were now emboldened, and some outcomes were staggering. Sheep were cloned. Stem cells grew into windpipes, urethras, and other organs. Stem cells also turned blood into skin. The Human Genome was sequenced. Personalized medicine began to match treatments to conditions, based on genetic profiles. In the social sciences, some conditions which were long recalcitrant (depression, OCD, dystonia, and dyslexia) now responded to new environmental interventions. The power of human intentionality was underscored. Almost every day, impressive new findings are posted on the web.

Out of this flurry of work, the concept of "plasticity" emerged. (It is also called "neuroplasticity", in reference to brain cells.) Plasticity heralds that we are changeable, adaptable, pliable beings, with the ability to morph into something more under the right circumstances. Yes, it's true that we're tied to the basic DNA building blocks that we inherited, but there's also much we can do to activate, extend, expand, enhance and improve ourselves by manipulating the environment—and rewiring that DNA. Humans are not simply hard-wired to perform in a certain way. They have input. They can help rewire themselves and their children.

Plasticity is huge. Great news! Somehow it just crept in on those proverbial "little cat feet." No announcements like with the iPad or the latest version of the iPhone. No parades. No drum rolls. No secret envelopes like the Oscars or Emmys—just the quiet outcome of years of laborious work and the insight of brilliant, hard-working scientists. Plasticity is one of the great tenets of the Knowledge Revolution and of our times, and it should change the way we all see ourselves. It carries a message of great hope and optimism. "Whoo Hoo! Three cheers for plasticity! Hurrah! Hurrah! Hurrah"! Shout it from the rooftops"!

Science journalist David Shenk, who tracked the emergence of plasticity and the new views of human potential, came to the following conclusion in his 2010 book, *The Genius in All of Us*:

> "Regardless of whether a child seems to be exceptional, mediocre, or even awful at any particular skill at a particular point in time, the potential exists for that person to develop into a high-achieving adult. Because talent is a function of acquired skills rather than innate ability, adult achievement depends completely on long-term attitude and resources and processes rather than any particular age-based talent quotient. While childhood achievement is, of course, not irrelevant (it's often a sign of early interest and determination), it doesn't rule any particular future success in or out."

These are encouraging words about an amazing concept! The power of the environment is such that every day, in every way, we are contributing to who we will become, and to an extent, to who our children will become. Furthermore, we can help decide this. No one knows one's own or another's limits.

One should take the long and incremental view. Some assume that if a child does not show early signs of precocity, he never will. Not necessarily. Still others will pull back and cease working with their child if he seems to lag behind. Another mistake. (I once had a neighbor who played ball outside with his son every day until he learned that the boy would not "start" on the Little League team. The father was bitterly disappointed, I heard—so much so that I never saw them out in the yard together again.) What a terrible waste of potential talent and a strike to a warm relationship. It's possible that with time and effort the child may have caught up or even overtaken the others in due course. No one knows how far one can go, until they try something wholeheartedly over the long course.

Within any individual child, the degree of plasticity will vary with age and stage. All children go through sensitive periods, when learning is easier. (Most of us know that the first two years are a boon to language development.) There are many others. It helps to know when these occur. A search of "Children's Developmental Benchmarks and Stages," on the internet will yield various sources to help you determine if your child is approaching or in a sensitive period. Also, an acute awareness of a child's natural proclivities, dispositions, interests and core talents is important. Learning will snowball when the best match is made between them and activities offered.

Be patient. Help your child to be patient. Slow steady increments of effort are what pay off. Like physical therapy or dieting, it's the long haul that counts. Many of us have seen how small changes can sculpt a body. The same is true of small increments of sustained effort in the arts, music, athletics, academics, and more. This is the basis of plasticity.

Many psychologists and neuroscientists believe that IQ can be boosted by twenty points, if not more. Twenty points is huge! This boost would take a person from the average to the gifted range. And Plasticity plays a role here.

Dr. Randy Jirtle at Duke University Medical Center compared each of our cells to a huge control board with lots of knobs and switches attached to our genes. Through our actions and free will, we can flip or turn those switches and knobs on or off to activate or suppress our genes.

When neurons (nerve cells) get excited, they create synapses, or electrical charges, exciting their neighbors and bringing them in on the action. This results in changes in the genes and a rewiring of the brain or organ involved. The extent and duration of the activity affects the degree of change. Some genes never become titillated and they wither or become pruned away. (Some of this is natural and a good thing, because it clears out the overgrowth; but sometimes it is not.) And we are the ones usually in charge. We can elect to throw certain switches or not. We can literally control the growth or contraction of our brains and bodies. And when we interact with others, we can help change them, too. Kids love to hear this.

"Hey. Want to be a little more musical? Here. Flip this switch." (A class of middle school kids were mesmerized to hear about human plasticity.)

"No. I want to be more athletic."

"Sure."

"Then turn that one over here." He points to the friend's kneecap.

As they laugh and mimic the switching actions, a more pensive student squints and asks: "You mean we're like orchestra conductors?"

"Exactly," the teacher says. " We can call forth certain sections to play when we want, and silence others, too… Picture yourself on the podium. You're in charge. Each of us is born to make beautiful music!"

Gross oversimplifications? In a sense. But not that far removed from reality either. An alternate explanation may go something like this:

Sometimes a smile, a hug, a word, or a song is enough to start the process whereby a gene is actually changed and hard wiring altered. This is what it may look like.: Words are spoken. An emotion arises or a sensation occurs. Bio-chemicals begin to flow. They flood specific areas of circuitry around the cells in the brain or other part of the body. The particles penetrate the permeable membrane of an affected cell, communicate with it, and persuade that gene to change ever so slightly. Neighboring genes may join in for the ride. The more repetitions of this process and the more genes affected, the greater the change that occurs. The deeper the pathways and the more sustained the action, the more lasting the impressions. It's an amazing process—plasticity in action.

The simplest action, such as reading this book, can go deep into our physiology, expanding our brain's real estate. It is not unlike how muscles build up in our bodies. Some call the mind a muscle. Some teachers teach this to their students: "The Mind is a muscle. If you use it, it will grow."

And this is what Carol Dweck and her colleagues taught a group of "at-risk" middle school students in New York City.

Sharing The Good News With Students:

In 2003, Dweck, psychology professor and her then-colleagues at Columbia University conducted a study with over five hundred seventh graders, who were preparing to take a high-stakes math test. All the students were low achievers, in math and also

15

lagging in motivation—but not for long—at least not half of them. The group was broken into two. One half of the students were given a mini-course on the brain. They were shown pictures and taught the basics of plasticity and how the brain functions. They were repeatedly reminded that the "mind is a muscle. If you use it, it will grow." During the marking period, they also prepared for the test in the usual fashion, drilling and so forth, but also repeated the mantra, "The mind is a muscle. If you use it, it will grow." They wrote and acted out skits about the brain, and learned to use visualization techniques. They imagined their brain cells chattering to each other as they stretched their limits and grew new gray matter. Though street-savvy in many ways, the students seemed amazed to learn this new content. "You mean I don't have to be dumb?" one of the lowest achievers asked the teacher, through eyes brimming with tears.

The second cohort of students also prepared for the high-stakes test, but did not learn about the brain, nor did they receive the mini-course on the brain's plasticity. They simply drilled and prepared in the usual time-honored way.

At the end of the marking period the same test was administered to both groups of students. The group who received the extra instruction on the brain scored significantly higher than the group who did not. (The student with the tears in his eyes went from a D-minus student to become a B-plus achiever that year.)

Like adults, kids can be skeptical unless you show them some proof. Perhaps it wasn't enough that teachers were telling students that practicing their math skills would help them achieve more. Maybe they needed that extra little piece of evidence that their hard work would pay off before they put in the effort; plus, they needed a dose of scientific proof and a greater familiarization with how their brains worked to prod them on.

Most people, including kids, tend to lean toward skepticism. They will be more apt to believe your motivational speeches, if you give them some proof. And parents can help, by giving them pep talks, or better yet, some specifics about how the brain works. Check any number of websites to brush up on your biology. Then share this with the kids. You might want to ask them to close their eyes and pretend they are neurons—excited about chatter from the neighboring genes. Have them visualize and act out what goes on in their brains when they work hard and are stimulated. Kids have no problem using their imaginations. They'll take it from there. For instance, I've seen students use water spritzers to replicate brain synapses—ZAP—"the nerve endings are talking to each other!" Through stimulation, the nerve endings are being rewired and growing together. This is how we build greater mental capacity.

So if plasticity is such good stuff, you may ask, why don't we hear more about it, and why don't more acknowledge it to take advantage of these powers? Good question. But the good news is that maybe they are. A scan of best-selling books, popular magazines, blogs, and public television schedules reveal an array of messages geared to encourage audiences to "listen up" on how to build better brains, bodies, immune systems, and relationships.

Still, everybody hasn't gotten the message. It's still popular to hide behind one's genes. How often have we heard: "I can't lose weight. My genes make me fat " or "I never could do math. I don't have the gene for it" or "My whole family lacks the music gene—we all have two left feet" etc., etc., etc. Hogwash! Some "mental housecleaning" needs to be done by a lot of people. If you're wise, and desire to be a good role model for your children, keep up to speed and embrace the new Knowledge Revolution. Reflect on your beliefs, and toss out any that are tangled up with old, outdated myths, such as the following:

Debunked Myths:

- **Intelligence is fixed.** FALSE. We now know that intelligence is not fixed. It is a process. Intelligence responds to the life we live. Anyone can grow smarter—or less smart depending on the life they lead. No one knows for sure the limits of their own or anyone else's intelligence. No one should allow anyone to put limits on themselves or their children.

- **If you're really smart, you don't have to work hard because truly smart people will just sail through new material.** FALSE. Brains and talent don't bring success. Effort and perseverance do. In fact, believing in intelligence or talent as something fixed and all-powerful can be detrimental to long-term success. Students, in particular, need to know this: Only people who have worked very hard make it to the top.

- **Genes determine who we are and what we will become in the future.** FALSE. We do not inherit traits directly from our genes. Instead we develop them through gene-environment interaction. Some believe that environmental factors may shape 80–90% of who we are.

- **We are given all the brain cells we will ever have at birth.** FALSE. We grow new brain cells until the day we die. True—there are periods of sensitivity, when it's easier to learn new material, but new learning can occur at any age. This myth was dangerous because it discouraged some adults from trying new things and gave too many parents the wrong impression that if their children didn't show early signs of precociousness, they probably never would. It's time for all to re-examine that prevalent belief because it isn't true.

- **Only active, conscious acts of learning make a difference.** FALSE. The majority of the activity affecting learning takes place at unconscious levels—including during sleep.

In summary, through the HAPS I was inspired to discover that we have much greater capacity for improving ourselves and developing talent in our children than we ever dreamed. Among other things, talent is developed over time.

- Talent is brought out by the environment, and parents are in control of much of that.
- Parents have the power to switch talents on or off in themselves and in their children.
- The brain is a learning machine that craves new learning. Parents can help speed up the way it processes sounds and sights.
- Many talented adults did not start out that way. (Conversely, many that did start out ahead, fizzled out.)
- It's important to believe in potential, and apply ongoing effort to evoke it.

It used to be that parents would look down at their newborns and wonder what they could become. Now they can look down at them and know that they, the parents, can write the script.

Chapter 2:
Belief Number Two: Effort

Effort and hard work are at the root of achievement, and hard work can offset lesser ability.

The belief that hard work coupled with enthusiasm, focused learning, and patience, are the components of success, was also prominent among HAPs.

This is the second bedrock belief shared by those savvy parents over the years. In addition to the expertise studies, beginning in the 1980's, others continue to back this up. A recent study conducted by Angela Duckworth at the University of Pennsylvania indicated that "grit" (perseverance and effort) corresponds to success more than almost anything else—more than SAT or ACT scores, more than IQ tests, more than any other standardized measure or intervention. These are strong results.

A Balance of Warmth and Authority is Ideal:

"I tell my kid hard work is the most important thing," said more than one Asian parent. "In order to succeed, you must put in the time and effort." And by placing a premium on effort, clear advantages accrued to those who held that belief. Jewish and Asian parents, in particular, preached this gospel. "If the early love is deep," one Asian mother asserted, "children will aim to please their parents… and when they feel that close attachment, they will want to keep that feeling going. As they discover that you value hard work, they'll begin to copy your example… They'll work hard with their school work so they don't let you down and break that strong bond." A Jewish mother agreed. Psychologist Sam Wang cites corroboration of this in the literature, and columnist David Brooks cites the famous Grant Study at Harvard, involving 268 students, as evidence that a warm childhood was very powerful.

In America, warm bonds are a linchpin of a movement called, "attachment parenting," which has been gaining ground in the past few years. Did you ever wonder where all these baby slings came from? Those and other tactile trends can be traced to the influence of Dr. James Sears and his popular book, *Attachment Parenting Book: A Commonsense Guide to Understanding and Nurturing Your Baby*—the first in a series—all equally popular. Attachment parenting advocates for breast feeding, co-sleeping, carrying the baby close to the body in a sling, and disallowing crying or extended periods.

In both the Asian and Jewish cultures, achievement is rewarded. Parents brag to grandparents and close friends, further tightening bonds. The roles of mothers are well-defined. The mothers hug a lot. The dads support the moms in their maternal role, which is generally highly regarded. Both groups shower the young with affection and lots of enthusiastic attention—all of which is believed to link to eventual high achievement; but is the establishment of a clear sense of authority. "Children need to know from the earliest years that the parent is the boss... so establish a few rules and enforce them," advised one Jewish parent.

Best-selling author Wendy Mogul agrees. In her book on Jewish parenthood, *The Blessing of a Skinned Knee*, Mogul states that "Children are not equal and they don't want to be... it just makes them feel insecure. It's important to start teaching children that you are the boss when they are very young, and to keep reminding them of that until they're old enough to leave home." "Honor thy father and thy mother," is instilled from an early age. Similarly,

Chinese parents make their line of authority clear. Children are taught that it is their duty to respect their elders and bring pride to the family. In her best-seller, *The Battle Hymn of the Tiger Mother,* author and Chinese tiger mother Amy Chuarecounted her personal experiences when she went overboard with the exercise of authority. Chua eventually learned to pull back and seek balance, but not without a cost.

Volition and Internal Motivation

Volition as the prime motivator of effort is always preferable. When a child is aware of the parents' love and authority in any culture and presented with the "carrot" a positive inducement voluntarily, he will be motivated to do his best. Effort will be high.

The "carrot" involves no pressure. No coercion. No fear of failure. It is the best way to learn. Its exact opposite, the "stick," on the other hand, involves overtones of threats and punishment. It is the worst way to learn. Sometimes the "stick" can have lasting deleterious effects.

When Dr. Fred Gage at the Salk Institute allowed a group of rats to exercise of their own volition, he saw their brains grow. On the other hand, a group of similar rats, who had to be prodded to exercise, did not perform as well, nor did their brains grow as much.

In his bestselling book, *Drive*, Dr. Daniel Pink of Harvard University noted that students who select their own projects are more motivated to excel than those who need to be constantly prodded.

You may recall that Bloom's 120 top achievers "fell in love" with their fields before mastering them. Only then did they commit to a grueling regiment of self-imposed hard work that drew them to the top of their respective fields.

Modeling

When parents work hard, kids usually work hard, too. There is an abundance of research that affirms that moods are contagious, and even small babies and tots, who love to mimic their parents, pick up their energetic vibes and strive to imitate their intensity and pace. Even when parents do not overtly appear energetic, but exude a type of undulating energy churning beneath the surface, little ones seem to pick it up and seek to model it. It's documented throughout the animal kingdom. It's observed in human beings. One of the best ways to get children to apply effort is to model it.

Pep Talks and Platitudes

Most of us use pep talks and platitudes to get our kids to work harder. Certain words just pop out of our mouths:

"That's the idea. Keep at it."

"Just keep your pedal to the metal."

"Your shoulder to the bar."

"Pull out all the stops.

"Kick butt."

"Crank it up."

"Never say die."

"Keep on truckin"

"Sparkle and shine."

"You got it. You got it. You got it. Go Girl."

"Great job. That's my gal. Keep at it." etc., etc., etc.

Parents of high achievers definitely do a lot of this sort of coaching. Sometimes they'll lace the drill with a pop tune: "No Retreat, Baby. No Surrender" (Springsteen,) or "Take it to the Limit... One More Time" (The Eagles) or "Don't Give Up" (Peter Gabriel), etc.

These songs can work wonders—especially if alternated with platitudes in more serious settings: "Way to Go, Linda. "Atta girl, Baby!" "That's my gal!" "Great job!" "Keep at it." "Bring it on home" (in excessive decibels); or they alternate with a more low-key approach—with good old-fashioned platitudes. The goal is the same—effort—but the energy level may vary. Some may call them trite and a little preachy, but they're certainly time-honored, and most agree they work:

"Effort builds character."

"Never give up."

"Chase your dream."

"An idle mind is the devil's workshop."

"Nothing worthwhile has ever been accomplished without hard work."

"Let nothing stand in your way. Nothing."

"If you fall, pick yourself up. Dust yourself off. And just go on."

"You learn from your mistakes."

"No matter what you want to do, you can do it—if you work hard enough."

"Follow your dreams," etc., etc., etc.

Yes, they are trite, worn, and preachy, but most parents swear by them. So do others. Politicians sprinkle their speeches with these clichés, as do many commencement speakers. One of my favorites was shared by the esteemed John Bogle, founder of the Vanguard Group, Inc. at a speech to a group of business students at Drexel University. He advised them to never let anything get in the way of their goals and to persevere. "Never give up," he said. "Never. Never. Never. Never. No. Never give up!" He explained that as a child he loved the children's book *The Little Engine That Could,* and begged his mother to read it over and over again to him. The message stuck. "It not only stuck," he said, "but it sustained me through many rocky turns in my work."

Of course, there are many other, more nuanced ways to draw effort out of your child, and some of these will be folded into the "Strategies" portion of this book. In the meantime, some have asked:

How Much Effort is Enough?

Author Malcolm Gladwell tells us that at a minimum, ten years or about 10,000 hours of back-breaking focused and guided work are needed to rise to the top of any field. He traces the trajectories of the Beatles, Bill Gates, and others as examples in his best-seller, *The Outliers* to illustrate that point. And those ten years weren't just years of plodding along. They were fueled by a dogged sense of determination and accompanied by backbreaking work, hectic schedules, clear spiraling goals and expert mentoring along the way. According to Gladwell, the ten years or ten thousand-hour rule pertains to all fields of endeavor.

"Not so," you may say. "I heard somewhere that Taylor Swift wrote *Our Song*, in twenty minutes, or that Elizabeth Gilbert wrote *Eat, Pray, Love*, in six weeks. They didn't pay their ten thousand-hour dues. They broke through to the top right in a snap." Wrong. While it's true that Swift and Gilbert ascended to the pinnacle of their fields rather quickly, they still put in the time. If one does the research, they'll learn that both ladies had been writing songs and books since childhood-- no less than ten years before they hit "paydirt."

And remember Mozart? Yes, he was exceptional at age four— but so were others—some even more so. But by the time Mozart was fourteen (ten years later—and after ten years of grueling practice, self-driven determination, and expert mentoring), Wolfgang Amadeus Mozart was finally composing works truly worthy of a musical "genius."

Are Some Kids Just Lazy?

A father brought that question up at a meeting. He had just heard about the "ten thousand-hour rule." He listened, then gasped: "Ten thousand hours? Man, I'm lucky if I can get ten minutes of work out of my kid. I guess he's just plumb lazy." Others nodded knowingly.

"I doubt it," a psychologist in the group responded.

"Lazy? Nah." He shook his head.

"A laid back temperament?"… Perhaps."

"Unmotivated?"… Hmm… Maybe.

"Physically or emotionally, challenged?"… Very possibly."

"The victim of bad habits? Another possibility."

"But sheer lazy?" he shook his head from side to side again, then paused.

"Very doubtful" he said soberly. "I don't think I've ever seen a truly lazy child … It goes against the grain of who and what a child is."

To encourage a hard worker, try some of the strategies offered here. If they work, fine. If they don't work, try some others. But never give up on a child. It's important to stay with him through disappointments and through all the years. Let him feel your support. If you're certain that the child has been challenged in topics related to his strengths and interests, and still isn't responding to anything, perhaps something *is* out of balance, and a conversation with your pediatrician may be in order. But don't rush to label him "lazy."

(An excellent book by Frank Lawlis, *Mending the Broken Bond,* offers tips to parents who feel the need to get back on track.)

And never underestimate the importance of balance. While beliefs in potential and effort are important, they alone are not enough. Extraordinary achievement is derived from a confluence of factors—physical, affective, cognitive and transcendent, interacting with one's genes in a balanced integrative sense.

Chapter 3:
Belief Number Three:
Balancing the Whole Child

Balance and attention to the Whole Child are essential to successful parenting.

We called them "Wonder Parents." You know the type. Almost too good to be true; good-looking, artistic, well-read, and the parents of three "Wonder Kids" who did it all. Danny was the eldest child—the envy of all the neighborhood. "Not only is he the best reader, writer, and runner in the class," my daughter informed me, "he's the only one who can really break-dance right." My son added that he was also "the only one in the neighborhood who could shimmy up onto Mr. Connor's roof to retrieve foul balls." I was duly impressed, of course, but I really liked the fact that he was also well-rounded, friendly, and truly a nice kid. He was generally obedient too.

But one hot summer night, as a group of us sat around the bonfire, chatting and tasting wine, Danny led the rest of the kids, whirling around the grounds, and swooping down on fireflies like dive-bombers, having the time of their lives. It was all good until they got too close to the bonfire. "Enough, kids," one parent admonished to what seemed to be a pack of stone-deaf children. No response. The frenzied pack whirled on. "Slow down," said another parent, then another, and another—all unheard, until Wonder Father finally looked up from his hosting duties and said sternly: "Danny, that's enough. Go inside and play a quiet game." Silence. The leader of the pack—Danny—came to a halt, and so did the others. The obedient boy lead them inside and soon emerged with cards and magic tricks, sitting quietly off to the side, to entertain his disciples for the rest of the evening. Not an "aw shucks" or "do we have to?' or a moan or groan from any of them. Danny showed them how to quickly change gears and settle down. Like his father, he had the touch. All the Wonder Family had the touch.

As I sat in Wonder Mom's kitchen the next morning, sipping cappuccino she had made with a fancy foam heart floating on the top, I asked her outright: "How do you do it all?"

"What?" she replied quizzically, blushing slightly.

"You know—run such an efficient home? You raise such happy, healthy, accomplished kids and so effortlessly. I pointed to her kids gleefully constructing a huge paper maché dragon in the next room. "Look at them. Creative and in-synch. Always. That's rare in many families. And you and your husband never seem to miss a beat."

"Not always," she shrugged. "We have our moments." I thought I saw her blush slightly. But I persisted.

"It all seems so easy. Surely you know we all admire you and your family. And I have to confess that we even call you the Wonder Family. Are you surprised?"

She smiled, looked down modestly, and poured more coffee, going around the foam heart, so as not to ruin the pattern. She must have known I wasn't leaving without an answer, for after a reflective moment she replied: "Love, of course. Lots of love." She must have sensed that I didn't think that was everything, because she went on. "I guess that's a given for all of us," she acknowledged, and went on. "So in addition, I'd have to say it's balance—balance and attention to the whole child: all aspects of the child—physical, affective, cognitive and transcendent. You've got to constantly keep your eye on all their needs."

30

"Tell me more."

She sighed. "It's hard work. Lots of hard work."

"What does that look like in the daily scheme of things?... How do you do that?" I was determined to learn this family's secrets. (This occurred around the time I had personally set out on a mission to learn all I could about drawing out the best in children, so I was truly primed.)

"You need to be constantly alert, pick up on their various needs," she responded. "It's definitely an ongoing challenge."

"Go on."

"You study them. Each one carefully. You plan activities. You weigh and measure what to leave in, what to leave out. You think about the intersecting dynamics. You talk to your spouse. You gauge: How much is enough? How much is too little?" She was really getting into it now. "My husband and I put our heads together a lot. Should we allow them to take this risk or that? Can we afford it? Whose needs come first? How will this affect the whole family? It usually comes down to something in the gut... We make decisions, and then we act on them."

"Yes. It does sound kind of hard. Very artful. How did you learn all this?"

"A lot is trial and error, I guess. Maybe it's an art... maybe it's a science." She rethought and reversed herself. "No... it's not a science. It's definitely not a science. There's no formula. No diagrams. No schematics. It's more like an art. You just try to wrap your head around each child—both the whole child and their distinct parts—and at the same time put them into the context of the whole family." At that moment, her husband entered the room and joined the conversation.

"That's right," he concurred. "We always try to consider the whole, and whether it's working. We talk about the 'wad.' If any part is out of whack, the whole—the wad—is probably out of whack, and we better see about it. For instance, if a child has a headache or a heartache or just seems frustrated or floundering with something, you know he's not going to be on his game, so we zero in on that first. We try to help him restore the balance to get him back on track. It's definitely an ongoing balancing act."

"We have different names for it," he laughed. "She calls it 'double Dutch.' I call it 'juggling.' Sometimes we both call it our 'little tango.' We do it a lot together."

She added, "The Tango is not so little sometimes… especially when you're trying to meet the needs of three kids—all so different."

"And please your partner at the same time, " he added. "Maybe that's why parenting is sometimes called life's toughest job."

I thought about it—especially the balancing part. It made sense. After all, we seek balance in our checkbooks, portfolios, social lives, diets, exercise routines, teams at the office, politics, and all aspects of our lives. So why not balance in parenting?

Later, at an evening discussion at the school, Wonder Father made this point:

"Is the whole child any different from any other system—a human body, an automobile, a band, an orchestra, a business or a corporation? All the parts need to be in synch, right? Otherwise, there's dissonance. Trouble. If any one part falters, so will the whole. Why not attend to the whole?"

Wonder parents had a great effect on many in our "crowd." They were my first real parenting models, and their comments predated what I would hear from many other wise and successful parents throughout the subsequent years.

Belief in the need to seek balance in parenting the "whole child" was a priority for them and became so for many of us. Eventually I noticed it was also the theme of some educational organizations: ASCD (Association for Supervision and Curriculum Development) and AASA (American Association of School Administrators) who regard the "whole child" as a major focus of their mission.

No one wants a lopsided child—accomplished in one area, but a train wreck in another.

Those *"Girls Gone Wild,"* and *"Boys Gone Wild,"* on TV, along with the misguided young celebrities and athletes played up in the media, have all somehow become lopsided. Someone forgot to monitor the "whole" in their upbringing.

"The whole truly is greater than the sum of its parts," advised parents from time to time and in a number of settings over the years. It was stressed with considerable passion. Think: a perfectly synchronized orchestra. That should be our goal.

In time, Wonder Parents moved away, but I never forgot the impression they made on me and our neighborhood peers. I'm grateful for the wisdom they imparted. To this day I can't watch *"Dancing With the Stars"* without being reminded of their "little tango," and thinking that they rated perfect "tens"—at least in my book.

Tracking the Whole Child:

Along the way, at one of the parenting meetings, an acronym for the facets of the whole child was created: "PACT." It stood for the Physical, Affective, Cognitive, and Transcendent realms—a quick and handy way to help us assess the domains. We began to think PACT:

> "P" is for the Physical realm—How fit is the body?
>
> "A" is for the Affective realm—How attuned are the emotions and the social landscape?
>
> "C" is for the cognitive realm—How engaged is the intellect?
>
> "T" is for the transcendent realm—How activated are the spirit and the sense of higher purpose?

If any were out of whack, we knew where our attention must go.

I liked the acronym PACT—then and now. Not only is it useful in monitoring the various aspects of a child's well-being, but to me, personally, it also implied a "compact"—a sacred trust between the Divine and the parents, who were graced with this child. Don't we all like to do our best to keep a PACT?

When I taught, I often used an imaginary PACT template to assess my students, as well as to take stock my own children, and even myself, personally, on occasion, if I sensed things were getting out of kilter.

Gradually I learned that some parents used PACT as a measuring stick at regular intervals. The intervals could vary:

The beginning of each school year

The start of each calendar year

Report-card time

Birthdays

The last day of school

The date of the annual physical exam, etc.

That made sense, too. Don't we schedule check-ups with our doctors and dentists on a regular basis? Don't we monitor our finances and taxes on a set schedule? Or bring in our cars for periodic check-ups and servicing? Why not keep a schedule to assess our kids?

Parents might ask:

"Are the kids on track in each area? If not, why not?"

"Are we putting too much emphasis on any one realm to the neglect of others?"

"Do we need to shift some attention and energy elsewhere?"

"Is it time to just monitor things, or should we ratchet up or ratchet down at this point— or even intervene drastically, if need be?"

"How do we fix some areas that are out of whack?"

Some parents involve their kids in the process of assessing wellness. One family noticed the kids were getting more sluggish than they liked, and in need of more physical activity. So the conversation went something like this:

"I've noticed some of us are more cranky than usual lately. Do you think it could be this spell of bad weather? Have we all just been cooped up too long?"

Heads nodded.

"Unfortunately, I hear there's more snow on the way. So what can we do to get ourselves moving and get out of our funk?"

The family brainstormed.

"Maybe we can dig out some old workout videos."

"Let's buy a new Wii cartridge."

"Maybe Mom can teach us Zumba."

"How about an afternoon or evening at the indoor driving range"

"Or the batting cage...?"

They tried a couple of different things and soon got back on the track.

Usually such conversations occur during family meetings, which some families hold on a regular basis—discussed under Strategy Fifteen.

"But if the issue is important enough, one family told me, we'll move offsite... go out to a simple but cozy little restaurant down the road or even to McDonald's to catch everyone's attention. This frees us up from distractions, and gives us more face time. It can work wonders for the team."

Attending to balance and the whole child doesn't mean that equal attention must be given to each domain. (Children's strengths often emerge in one area, and of course, it makes sense that this area will be front and center for a good bit of time. "Well-rounded" does not mean a complete orb. It is normal for the areas of strength to get extra attention at times. But no one single area should ever be neglected, as they all contribute and support the main strong suit in a different way.)

All the domains are interconnected and integrated. Each facet affects the others. We can't be chopped up into little bits because everything is connected, and a decline in one can adversely affect the others. Tending to the whole often fuels motivation, igniting a fire in the belly—and the desire to excel.

PACT helps us examine the parts of the whole in detail. PACT sets that up for us. In Part Two of this book, we'll address each of the domains in sections, but only for the sake of discussion. We must remember that they can never be truly disentangled.

There are many ways to parent a child, and there is no right or wrong way—any more than there is a right or wrong way to coach or teach or interpret art or literature or music.

But the three belief systems described here—beliefs in potential, effort, and balancing the whole child—have been pivotal to the cohort of successful and happy parents I have known. Together they form a firm foundation and the basis for the strategies which we'll now discuss.

Part 2

Forty-Five Strategies for the Domains

◆ ◆ ◆

Through the years, I've observed the following:

- Some parents believe in potential but don't know what to do.
- Some parents know a little, but aren't sure it's worth the effort. ("After all, don't genes make most of the calls?")
- And some parents just don't care. Basically overwhelmed, they don't have the time or energy to give to parenting.

And then there are the HAPs. The HAPs believed in potential. They applied ongoing effort and they sought to balance the needs of the whole child. They were full of strategies and ideas about how to do this. The next chapters outline these.

There were far more than these forty-five strategies, but these stood out by the degree of passion, intensity and frequency with which they were shared. Some HAPs emphasized them because they were commonly overlooked or underaddressed by peers, and that irked them. They wished more parents would hone in on them more closely. The forty-five strategies were also vetted by research. One may call them "tried and true." For simplicity's sake, they are organized under the major domains of the child: physical, affective, cognitive and transcendent—but again, they work best when integrated as a whole. That's how humans function best—holistically.

I've have received so much input for this book. I'm grateful to the many parents who weren't afraid to stand up at meetings and share their feelings and opinions openly and those who took pains to meticulously lay out their children's developmental histories. I appreciate also the rich and colorful stories they shared.

Some strategies are age-specific, and the reader may be inclined to skip over them, but that may be a mistake. Generally speaking, we develop spirally. One stage affects the others. ("Infant bonding," for example, obviously refers to babies, but embedded in this concept are insights and lessons that affect humans of all ages—e.g. touch, deep gazes, reciprocity, etc., that go on making a difference at any age. Alternately, the strategy "knowing the system," applies to older school-age children, but some may be helpful to parents of younger children, who wonder about what lies ahead.) The vast majority of strategies are age-neutral, and can be ratcheted up or down to apply to many stages. With the three beliefs as a foundation, the forty-five strategies offer a balance of opportunities for all ages.

Don't be intimidated by the length of some lists. They are not meant to be mandates—just menus to choose from. Consider any that speak to you and your child's personal needs. I would urge you, though not to completely skip over any one domain, for the four domains work best when they interlock. Select a few interventions at first. Then come back later for more, if you wish. Remember, progress comes in small, slow, steady increments over time. If you only have time for one or two, that is better than none at all. Above all, savor and enjoy these childrearing years. They are truly a gift!

Chapter 4:
The Physical Domain

INTRODUCTION:

There's certainly something about the physical presence of a baby that gets everyone's attention. So small. So perfect to scale. So tightly packed with power—capable of making grown people quiver, even weep, at its first revelation. It is magnificence personified! Then you immediately start to wonder, "What do I do with all this?"

All aspects of the physiological are all so closely aligned to the mind, emotions, and spirit, that it seems an impossible bundle. A bit overwhelming! So, when they place that mysterious and magical bundle into your arms, you know this is big. You sense it in every fiber of your being, and the two of you resonate. Your world shifts. You know you'll never be the same. And that's when you ask, "Now what?"

◆　◆　◆

Strategy 1:

STRONG INFANT BONDING

Get this one right, and almost
everything else will fall into place.

Most parents used to think that tending to the physical side of the child was the easy part of parenting—far less complicated than the emotional side. If the baby was wet or cold or hungry, there were diapers, blankets, and bottles or breasts to address the needs—but not so with emotions. They seemed so complex and ethereal. Emotions were hidden from view. So were the intellect and the spirit. But the body—the physical domain—that was right out there. Straight-forward and easy to read. This was good.

"Just take that slimy, slippery bundle home," they implied at the hospital. "Wash him off, wrap him up, keep him dry and feed him. He'll be just fine... Later, yes, you'll play with him— talk and read together. Give him a few toys, games, fresh air, and exercise. And you'll see that he'll begin to blossom on his own." There wasn't much else that parents needed to do to bring the baby along.

The medical community advised parents to "allow the little blossoms to bloom on their own schedules." As recently as the '60's and '70's, newborns were pretty much regarded as little eating, pooping, sleeping machines, who in due course would grow and develop as they were pre-wired to do. And when in doubt, there was always Dr. Spock.

Then science and technology teamed up. New gadgets for imaging began to emerge, changing that view: "Why, it's astounding... the brain appears malleable—a lot less stiff than we thought. It responds to all kinds of things," experts concurred. The conclusion was that babies were really like little geniuses after all—not automatons, as assumed, but capable of learning sooner and better than ever imagined. Advice took an about-face. The implication was that maybe parents ought to step it up a bit—fertilize and stimulate those little blossoms. Exercise those little bodies. Play lots of music, and fill the air with interesting sights and smells. Get those synapses firing, and rev up those tiny neurons post haste. Yes, as mentioned, in the late 1970's and into the 1980's, there was a distinct change in the air, and parents had reason to take on more responsibility.

There was renewed interest in the parenting role, too—lots of talk about oxytocin and prolactin (satiation and cuddle hormones, important to the newborn). Physical bonding and its long-term effects took front and center. We learned from "America's pediatrician," T. Berry Brazelton, that children who bonded well with the mother later performed better in school. They also formed stronger human relationships. This advice was a far cry from the casual laissez-faire approach that had preceded it. And today strong bonding with physical closeness remain a prominent focal area for parents of all young children— newborns, in particular. As one diligent and informed parent said, "Get this one right and almost everything else will fall into place."

By the 1980's, many parents had caught on. It was no longer appropriate to view one's baby as a little automaton—awaiting to blossom. "Let's work with him," many said. "Let's awaken the senses. Science has shown that we can do much to secure strong, intimate, emotional attachments."

Bonding was now said to be best when Mom and Dad (and especially Mom) were actively engaged in introducing baby to the world in a positive sense. Bonding (sometimes called "attachment") came to be regarded as critical to healthy development. It occurs when Mom and baby "click."

Some of the physical components of bonding are:

Touching
Nursing
Direct and prolonged eye contact
Stroking
Nuzzling
Kissing
Hugging
Rocking
Speaking
Singing
Humming

Smiling
Laughing
Tickling
Cooing
Frowning
Pointing
Playing give and take
Dancing
Peek-a-Boo
Tapping and drumming
Exposure to various sensate experiences and stimuli

Some of the subtleties may matter most. Experts are now fairly specific in this regard:

- The baby should be put to the mother's breast. The touch, smell, and warmth will be reassuring. Then comes the Gaze, with the baby instinctively gazing back—drilling down, learning about Mom, and each connecting with the deepest part of their being. (Sometimes the Gaze can be overlooked. This is not desirable.)

- Ideally, the mother will sustain the Gaze, even though some babies will whimper and look away. This is the beginning of an important and intimate new relationship.

- Mom and Dad should repeat the Gaze from time to time, varying it slightly. They should begin to talk, and actually carry on a conversation with the baby. We cannot rule out that even the youngest baby is attuned to the love imparted in this communication. As the weeks pass, change expressions and tones. Begin to observe what pleases and displeases the baby, and respond accordingly.

- Parents should mimic the subtleties of baby's actions. Echo his sounds. Squeal if he squeals. Pout if he pouts. Blink when he blinks. Mirror all his facial expressions.

- Sway with the baby—ever so lightly. Talk to him. Hold him up and pierce deeply into his eyes. Babble on. Tell him he is the king of the universe.

- Be careful not to over-stimulate. Play. Rest. Play. Rest. Play. Rest. Babies and young tots need lots of sleep to process their new environment.

As the baby grows, the scenarios enrich:

- Roll around the floor. Play with the baby. Use rhythm. Talk and sing a lot.

- Vary sensory stimuli—aromas, tastes, textures. Try different toys. When you find one he absolutely adores, buy variations of the same thing, and make notes of his preferences. Someday, you'll share this with him and he'll be amazed and appreciative that you took the time to do this.

- Floor time is particularly delightful to toddlers. Romp and roughhouse a bit—even with the girls. Continue to follow their lead. If he loves dinosaurs, invent new species. Cover yourself with a sheet, and roar out their names. If your daughter loves princesses, put on a bathrobe and rescue her from the "tallest tower ever." Make a fool of yourself. That is part of what bonding is.

- Expose the baby to lots of music. Studies show that its effects can reach far into the future. Music enhances reasoning skills that underpin math, engineering and other disciplines.

- Pour on the language. Talk, coo, sing, and read. High pitched "parentese" is particularly interesting to the young baby. Language not only stimulates imagination and offers new knowledge, it paves the way for acquisition of spiraling sophisticated ideas. Read to the baby every day—at first for brief intervals, then for longer ones. Interest is key. Surf the net and comb the stores or garage sales for their favorites. Play with voices. Make funny faces. Create special effects.

- Be responsive, but not 100% of the time. No one can do that, and sometimes, it's best to let the baby self-soothe. Let the baby fuss at times until he leans that he can calm himself down or entertain himself. This is a very important requirement, because it is a precursor to delayed gratification, which in turn experts tell us is later associated with superior learning and character formation. Babies should not be allowed to cry for extended periods, though.

How much responsiveness versus self-soothing is too much? These are judgment calls. One never wants to let a baby cry for too long a period—or heaven forbid, whip himself into a frenzy. But, of course some fussing is normal and should be expected and allowed. If he's fed and dry and warm and otherwise comfortable and wants to fuss, let him fuss. He and you will soon learn that he can calm himself down. I guess these are some of the "juggling," "double Dutch," "tango" routines that Wonder Parents alluded to. Sometimes you just have to go with your gut. There is no template.

Bonding is physicality of the highest order. There is no way of knowing how many switches are flipped and knobs turned on in the bonding process—possibly billions or trillions or even more. These are the days and months of greatest growth, and greatest plasticity.

Bonding is both simple and complex—messy and frustrating—but also warm and wonderful, starting them off on the right foot and connecting them for life. And the body remembers. It absorbs all aspects of bonding, and remembers them on some level—the tenderness, the love, the gentle touches, the warmth. It is stored in there—somewhere, somehow, within the child forever. (It may help new parents to remember this at the 2:00 A.M. feeding.)

46

Children who do not experience satisfactory bonding can suffer long-term consequences. In the 1980's, thousands of Romanian orphans were left to languish in their cribs, and now are noticeably affected by a variety of physical and mental disabilities.

Pediatrician William Sears and his wife Martha, have authored a series of very popular parenting books that advocate a style called "attachment parenting." The first and most popular of the books is *Everything You Need to Know About Your Baby from Birth to Age Two*. It highlights three notable practices of attachment parenting: breastfeeding, carrying baby close to the parents' body in a sling, and sleeping very close to the baby. While parenting is a personal matter, from any angle, bonding (or "attachment") is a big deal—a big big deal, and worthy of your full attention.

◆　◆　◆

Strategy 2:

The Gaze

There's so much more in the Gaze than most parents realize. The eyes truly have it.

The eyes have a language of their own. From the moment of birth to the mutual celebration of some feat, the eyes bring you together with your child.

"Mom. Mom. Look at me. Watch me." In her cute little Speedo swimsuit, and her tiny bronzed body, she trembles with excitement as she gets ready to dive off the high platform—a move she never ventured before. She now catches sight of Mom's Gaze and gets up enough courage. Swish! When she bobs out of the water, her eyes immediately scan to meet Mom's.

"Yes. Yay! I saw that," Mom signals with a smile, a wave and a thumbs-up. "It was terrific. You're the greatest." But it is not only Mom's voice, but mostly her eyes that carry the real message. It's what some call the Gaze—that deep knowing look that drills down to the soul or electrifies a child at various moments. It's a variation on that same gaze that bonded them together in the seconds after birth—still sharp and on-target as a laser beam. It has a way of reassuring and sometimes even piercing to the child's core. Something similar will be repeated countless times, in various contexts through the years. Each time, the child draws affirmation and strength from the visual connection.

A lot of parents overlook the power of the Gaze, but those who don't, swear by its effectiveness. We all know how important it is to make eye contact when first introduced to a stranger, or a business associate, or to cement an existing relationship. Maybe we know of a torrid love affair that began with a deep gaze— either personally or through a movie—or of friendships that may have gone by the board due to a hostile, ill-timed or misplaced gaze. But do we appreciate what we have when we use it with our children? Not always. Savvy parents do, though. It helps to be intentional with the Gaze.

"I always make sure I give him the Gaze when he's performing on the field or on the stage, or wherever he is at a special moment," a father said. "Sometimes others are talking to me and it's easy to become distracted, but I try to make sure I make eye-contact with my child at the right point. I want him to know that the link is there. Dad's with you all the way! One hundred percent. The Gaze says it without sharing any words. My eyes carry that to him."

Experts tell us the power of the Gaze begins at birth. Galinsky says, "All newborn babies instinctively look Mom in the eye. If

Mom responds by gazing deeply into baby's eyes, the baby appears satisfied—affirmed. But if Mom looks away, researchers have documented sadness, and possibly signs of agitation in the baby. This is no small thing. Those signs will remain until a reconnection occurs." T. Berry Brazelton adds that "eye-to-eye contact serves the purpose of giving a real identify or personification to the baby, as well as getting a rewarding feedback from the mother." If this does not occur, it is "lost opportunity." That first Gaze is critical—an opportunity not to be overlooked.

Have fun with the baby and the Gaze. Squint. Roll your eyes back and forth and around in your head. Blink rapidly. Move your eyebrows, Groucho Marx style. The "eyes" will have it. Never underestimate what the baby is taking in. Genes are activated and expressed at an enormous rate during those early days and months.

As baby grows, the eyes can sometimes be used to discipline. Without a word they can say, "No, you may not have another piece of candy." "No, put that expensive glass bowl down." Or "If you don't stop racing around this restaurant you'll be grounded for a month." The French have a name for this mode of the Gaze. They call it "The Eyes," and according to author Pamela Druckerman, it's a prominent part of French discipline.

I recently witnessed one father use "the Gaze," to discipline his child at a local Walmart. The child who wanted a new toy, was slipping into full meltdown mode in front of a huge group of holiday shoppers----you know the act—squirming and kicking and slinking to the floor in the crowded aisle. The father crouched down and looked straight into the boy's eyes, and said, "No. The answer is no." As he spoke, the father placed his hand gently and calmly on the child's crown and held it there for a moment. I saw him drill deeply into his son's eyes. For a fleeting moment, the child seemed hypnotized. "No," the father repeated. The combination of the Gaze and touch worked wonders. The boy calmed down and the two went merrily on their way.

The Gaze holds its power throughout life. Older children need the Gaze—sometimes for discipline, sometimes for affirmation, sometimes, just to show that you care.

At a meeting, one parent of teenagers shared how she used the Gaze to send out caring signals, even to their backs.

"I use a lighter version to watch them until they are out of sight," she said. "Whenever I drop them off at school or a friend's house or at the mall, I watch them carefully until they disappear. I gaze at their backs. And I know they feel my eyes upon them, wishing them well, praying that they're kept from harm. I want them to feel their personal guardian angel, watching over them. Sometimes, they turn around to make sure I'm still watching them. I think they feel the Gaze on their backs. They never said it, but I think they like it. I know they sense my love." The Gaze is a powerful thing.

The full power of the Gaze may be conferred best during poignant moments. Maybe a teen is pouring out his heart after breaking up with a girlfriend, or has just been turned down by his top college choice. Or a pre-teen has just been cut from the team, or has especially good news to share—a high honor or award. A soulful Gaze at that poignant moment can say it all. You'll cement your deepest pride or empathy. They will know of your unconditional love. The Gaze doesn't always need words to accompany it. It can say, "I feel for you," or "I am here for you," or "I am so proud that you are my child" with just the eyes. The Gaze is sometimes better than words alone.

> The Gaze is a Swiss army knife of expressions with diverse applications that should not be underestimated.

Like all tools, it works best with practice. So sharpen it. Cultivate it. Discover its broad range of purposes. You'll sense when it feels right, and you'll be glad you've mastered the Gaze.

◆　◆　◆

Strategy 3:

The Touch

One never outgrows the need for touch. A teenager will need the warmth of your touch as much as a baby.

Like the Gaze, the Touch, is another physical "outreach," too often underutilized. "People in America don't touch enough, " Dr. Ashley Montagu shared at a conference in Wilmington, Delaware. I remember that day well. The tall English anthropologist wowed the crowd with his wisdom, experience and humor. "I don't know why," he said, "but Americans seem to fear the touch—almost as much as the people in my own country do." When the laughter died down, he took on a more serious tone. "This is a mistake. A really serious mistake. And totally unnatural in the animal world. All living creatures need touch. They cannot survive without it, and they certainly can't thrive." He went on to use the example of kittens deprived of touch by mother cats, who for some reason refuse to groom, lick or cuddle their young. When this happens, the kittens cannot eliminate. Then they perish. The same happens with other animals.

In his landmark book, *Touching: the Human Significance of the Skin*, Montagu goes on to say that of all the senses, touch seems to be the most powerful to the baby. It not only fosters emotional connections, but increases the baby's cardiac output, promotes respiration, discourages lung congestion and helps the baby's gastrointestinal functions. The movement of rocking helps digestion and absorption of food. Positive touch lowers the stress hormone, cortisol. (Too much cortisol can damage young brains.)

Montagu's strong feelings about the importance of touch were echoed by immigrant parents from time to time. "In my country," a Chinese mother stated "newborn babies don't go home from the hospital before the mother learns 'Tuina,' the art of baby and child massage. Every mother is taught that skill." "And in my country," a Cambodian father added, "Touch goes on at all ages. In fact, it's not unusual to walk down the street and see two businessmen holding hands. It's a totally natural thing—just a simple sign of friendship. But not in America. Can you imagine what your banker would think if you grabbed his hand while you were walking down the street?"

"In Japan, we believe in holding the child very close for the first three years," said a Japanese mother. "We give them lots of hugs and kisses, and spend as much time as possible with them. We feel this strengthens the bond, and makes the child more apt to please the parents… and to become more teachable, too. Western parents seem in such a rush to have their kids grow up. They want them independent very quickly. They don't hold them close enough and long enough in my judgment." A study by Kochanska, Philibert, and Barry confirms this.

Many researchers have studied the effects of touch in humans at all stages of life—birth to death—perhaps nowhere more intensively than by Tiffany Field and her colleagues at the Touch Research Institute in Florida.

According to Fields, touch does the following:

- facilitates weight gain in preterm infants
- enhances attentiveness

- alleviates depression
- reduces pain
- reduces stress hormones
- improves immune function (Touch Research Institutes. Field et al., 1986)

It is understandable, then, that thousands of Romanian orphans, deprived of touch and left to languish in their cribs in the 1980's bear permanent mental, physical and emotional scars.

The body remembers, it seems not only what it experiences, but what it fails to experience. Sensate responses are stored within. Positive ones foster physical and emotional health. Negative sensate responses can create emotional blockages, many of which may require touch, and/or talking therapy to resolve years later. The subtleties of touch are impossible to measure, but more and more believe they seep into one's subconscious and play a role in the wellness of the whole person.

But it's important that young children receive guidance in discerning good touch from bad touch. A highly effective long standing program, "Good Touch, Bad Touch," has evolved and is now called: "Child Help—Speak Up—Be Safe." The program can be used by parents and teachers to help teach their children about this sensitive topic. Some schools use it in their health or developmental guidance programs. You may want to inquire about it.

Of course, it is always best if children learn "good touch" from their parents in a natural way. One parent talked about her habit of giving bear hugs to her kids—including her two teenagers, before they go out the door. "I hug them, and tell them that they are mine, and that I love them. They put on the 'Oh Mom,' face, but I don't care. Deep down I know they like it. Sometimes my husband even gives what we call, Daddy Bear Hugs. I think if we stopped, they'd be upset."

New York Times' columnist, David Brooks describes the memory of the effects of some simple touch he experienced during horseplay with friends, years in the past—in high school. His friends pressed him good naturedly into his locker, and he claims he can still vividly recall the exact feel and effects of that occurrence. Though the touch occurred some forty years ago, it was as if it were yesterday. Touch goes much deeper than most of us realize.

Children never outgrow their need for warmth and a caring touch.

Simple ways that parents can confer love and keep that bond intact through touch are:

- Wrestling and jostling
- Patting them on the shoulder or back
- Giving "high fives"
- Exchanging "fist bumps"
- Sitting close to them on the sofa to watch TV
- Snuggling while reading to younger children
- Sitting close to play video games with older ones
- Giving back, hand, or shoulder massages
- Holding or grasping their hands
- Combing, braiding hair, or styling hair
- Giving manicures and pedicures
- Hugs
- Kisses

Keep up the talking and the touching. While most parents "get" the talking part, a lot forget to touch. Yet, coupled with "The Gaze," touch can be dynamite."

◆ ◆ ◆

Strategy 4:

Encouraging Exploration

Let them run down long corridors—traverse open fields—explore sprawling beaches. Let them think the universe is theirs—just for the taking.

It's only after they've had their fill of free-wheeling, oxygen boosting, exhausting workouts, that they're ready to settle down anyway. That feeling that the world is theirs to command dies off too soon for most. What happens to that fearlessness-- that feeling that the whole world is yours to seize and devour?

Who wouldn't agree that the world is sorely in need of more bold leaders who still feel those rhythms—the risk takers with endless courage and inquisitive and determined minds?

What would we give for more of them—adults who have never fully outgrown those childish and exploratory inclinations? Bold people. Courageous people. Creative people with lingering curiosity and the willingness to explore new horizons. There are still some around, of course. But not nearly enough. Former Pennsylvania Governor, Ed Rendell, bemoans this in his 2012 book, *A Nation of Wusses: How America's Leaders Lost the Guts to Make Us Great*. He asks what will we do in this world when no one is left who is willing to step up and take chances—to show us the way?

But thankfully Mother Nature gives us fresh starts in each new life. Even the tiniest baby loves to explore. Just observe him for a minute: "What's this dotted yellow creature dangling over my crib? Maybe I can swat it. I wonder what this blanket tastes like? Feels like? Smells like? And what makes this rubber toy squeak? Let me crawl on over to that furry creature purring funny sounds and take a bite out of it."

Psychologist John Medina says "Babies learn about their environment through a series of increasingly self-corrected ideas. They experience sensory observations, make predictions about what they observe, design and deploy experiments capable of testing their predictions, evaluate their tests, and add that knowledge to a self-generated growing data base. They use fluid intelligence to extract information, then crystallize it into memory. Nobody teaches infants how to do this, yet they do it all over the world. They are scientists, as their parents suspected all along. And their laboratory is the whole world."

At first, parents find this cute. But as baby branches out and flirts with danger, some parents don't think it's so adorable anymore.

"Eeek! Don't go near that. Stay away. You'll get hurt. Come back here. Come here to Mommy… Where's the playpen? Honey, put him in the playpen, please. He's going to get hurt—(Code: He's also tearing up the house)… Oh, I'm so exhausted!"

In some homes, all the child hears is the big No!

"No. You can't climb those stairs."

"No. You can't run down that hallway."

"No. You can't go camping out in the woods—or to that friend's house with the five dogs, or horseback riding, or to the mall, or to the rock concert or on public transportation or on the foreign exchange trip. No. No. No."

"Too much trouble. Too unsafe. Too unnecessary. Too expensive. Too much effort, and definitely too much wear and tear on my nerves." Simply too much! Period. End of discussion. (Much of this is usually unspoken, of course.)

A parent should always try to weigh the benefits against the risks before saying "No."

Pause and reflect. Can reasonable limits be imposed without dousing the spirit? Are there any benefits to allowing a longer leash? Certainly, safety must come first, but if that is not a major issue, some prudent risks should be allowed—even encouraged.

Author Gever Tulley tell us there are at least "Fifty Dangerous Things You Should Let Your Children Do" in his book by that name. He suggests that we build competent children by giving them opportunities to distinguish those things that are truly dangerous from those which merely contain an element of risk. And taking risks can be a good thing for children's healthy growth, he assures us. "The best way is to introduce them to risk through measured, supervised exposure," he says. Brace yourself, because depending on the age, Tulley suggests that parents allow the child to do the following:

Throw a spear.

Burn things with a magnifying glass.

Spend an hour blindfolded.

Make a slingshot.

Deconstruct an appliance.

Learn tightrope walking.

Lick a nine volt battery.

Explode a bottle in the freezer.

By allowing dangerous things, Tulley says, kids will be *more* safe, because such activities will teach children how to explore safely, how to judge danger, and how to predict where the hidden snags may reside. This sets them on the path to exploring on their own.

Of course, we have a new generation of helicopter parents among us, who are probably choking by now. Given their instincts, they'll never cut the child loose, nor allow any of the above. They will continue to stand at attention or hover, waiting to receive or respond to the next media report on imminent dangers and threats. It's a wonder more kids aren't raised in bubbles! Whatever happened to our parents' advice: "Go out and play, kids, and don't come home until it's dark outside?" I understand that times have changed, and certainly safety must always come first. But don't forget to reserve some measure of "GO FOR IT!" to round out the Whole Child, and to preserve that God-given exploratory instinct, that could save the universe some day.

If you suspect you're an overly cautious parent, ask yourself these questions:

- How important is it to me to have a child who seizes the world by the tail?

- Am I, myself, a curious person? Or am I overly-cautious?

- Do I possess the joy of discovery and awe?

- Do I hear more "no's" than "yes's" coming out of my mouth?

- Is time always an issue for me? Am I chronically hurried?

- Do I sometimes follow the child's lead in seeking new vistas?

- Do I initiate new experiences?

- Do I show overt excitement at new discoveries?

- Are babysitters, grandparents and other caregivers put on "short leashes?"

- Do I signal "go for it," if the terrain seems safe and the child seems interested?

- If safety dictates that the answer must be "No," do I patiently explain "why?"

If the answer to most of these questions is "no," it may be time to rethink this aspect of your parenting style. Exploration is basic to transcendence and critical to intellectual and emotional development—not to mention the longevity of the universe.

◆   ◆   ◆

Strategy 5:

Eye-Hand Coordination

There's pleasure as well as challenge in getting those little fingers to fly across a project at just the right speed.

Activities that foster eye-hand coordination have considerable neurological benefits, according to scientists. Every time you peel a potato, or braid your hair, or knit a scarf, or finger a tune on the piano, your brain thanks you. They are not all on the same level, of course, but they all add value to your circuitry. Unfortunately, not all parents realize or appreciate this. When Amy Chua published her now-famous tome, *Battle Hymn of the Tiger Mom*, she besmirched arts and crafts, as nothing but Fluff. Fluff. Fluff. Not worth the time of day. Piano? Okay, nice. Permissible. Math? Yes, it befits a scholar. Other hard core academics? Definitely on the radar. But arts and crafts? No. Never. They're simply a waste of time—valuable time that otherwise could be redirected to getting ahead.

Amy was wrong on this count because science's scans have affirmed that even the simplest manual tasks can add neurological and cognitive value. Not only does the brain have to figure out which muscles to contract in which order, and how much pressure to bear on what specific areas, it also has to estimate the placement of the fingers and follow the task at hand carefully with the eyes. And I don't mean just playing a musical instrument. Any time the eyes and hand work in coordination, the child improves, and the child grows in discipline, self-control, focus, concentration, and attention skills—bases for cognitive growth.

Perhaps to Amy and others, though, arts and crafts are synonymous with relaxation, mindless "kicking-back," activities that encourage the brain to turn to mush. But to the contrary. "Getting ahead" requires relaxation. What's that they say about "all work and no play… ?" It's true. The best formula for the mind and body seems to be a balanced schedule: Work. Play. Rest. Work. Play. Rest. Eye-hand activities of various sorts can fit in very well with that formula. Athletes, physical therapists and others know the regiment well. But not all appreciate it.

Some scientists suggest that the connections between the eye and the hand and the brain are so important that they may have stimulated the evolution of our species. One such hypothesis was first put forth in none other than the Buddhist *Tao* (Chapter 10B), which speculates that the reason for the development of man's larger brain and stronger hands is a result of our ancestors' tool-making ability—rather than the other way around. But regardless of the historical sequence, the power of the intersections of eye, hand, and brain remain strong.

In my experience parents of accomplished children beat a steady path to art centers, camps, playgrounds, scouts, youth clubs, Sunday Schools—anywhere that handcrafts were offered, and those eyes and hands can coordinate projects. Their homes were often filled with the by-products. Many grace my own home—my personal favorite is a bird carved out of driftwood, and sitting on my coffee table.

If you're still not convinced of the creative energy generated by crafts, walk through your local A.C. Moore, Michael's or other craft store. Aside from Apple Stores, (always bursting with palpable energy), you'll feel the energy and creativity bouncing off the walls. If that's not convenient, try something else:

Take a quick walk down memory lane—recall the unique aura of—raffia, cellophane, pipe cleaners, crepe paper, paste, glue, clay, paper mache, feathers, etc. Remember how they smelled and felt—the joy of experimenting? They drew something out of you. Each had its own sensate appeal—an open invitation to create and imagine new possibilities—firing up those neurons and expanding neuronal real estate. Never underestimate the value of that eye-hand exchange!

Music is another area that expands the brain as it gets the fingers flying, (and an area where even Chua, and the experts are in agreement). Not only is playing a musical instrument highly desirable for any child, its benefits often spill over to other areas. "Playing the trumpet helps keep my daughter sane," one high school mother commented. "She's involved in so much, but this seems to bring her stress level down. Since she also plays in the marching band, it also gives her a social life—as well as some extra physical activity." (If one adds in the transcendent perks, I guess you could say music is an ideal activity to elicit and help balance all aspects of that student's PACT.)

"But wait," as they say in the infomercials: "There's more. That's not all." There are other ways to maximize the eye/hand advantage.

Household chores and jobs around the home also exercise the brain as they advance manual skills. A healthy dose should be folded into a child's routine—for more reasons than one. They also contribute to teamwork and enhance the family unit. The cooking, cleaning, bed-making and car washing, etc., that goes on between other activities, builds functional skills and personal independence as it deepens circuitry. So does sweeping floors, sorting laundry, sanding furniture, shucking corn, peeling carrots, cutting up fruit, grooming and caring for pets, planting and watering and weeding gardens, setting the table—all those activities which Chua and others probably eschew in favor of the steady beat of the academics.

Those wise parents who seek balance and encourage chores, sometimes pay allowances to their children, but not all. The parents who do pay, feel it sweetens the pot. One dollar a week for each year of the child's age seems to be the norm today. Therefore, a six year old would get $6.00, if the family can afford it. Others don't pay, believing that doing chores is just part of being on the family team. There's no set rule. Whichever route a parent chooses is fine, as long as they don't totally overlook chores as an opportunity for growth. There's much more there than meets the eye—and hand.

◆ ◆ ◆

Strategy 6:

Exercise

Jack be nimble. Jack be quick. By the way, "How did Jack get so quick?" Simple. He moved.

Exercise did not always command the respect that it does today. I remember one parent, years ago, practically on her hands and knees, pleading for the principal to excuse her very bright daughter from gym: "Please, please, pulleez. She's not good at gym, and it doesn't suit her. All those silly exercises get her upset. And those icky little uniforms. She just can't abide them. They take their toll on her self-esteem. You and I know she's brilliant and she doesn't need gym. It's a waste of her precious time. She's on the track to a Nobel Prize, so why not let her use her time more productively? We can't all be good at everything, can we? And gym just does not work for her."

Sadly the principal caved. With a wink of the eye, and a wave of the hand, the girl was dismissed early on gym days—presumably to sit on the couch and eat Twinkies as she poured over her physics books. That mindset was not uncommon years ago. Very bright kids didn't always have the same demands placed on them. But after awhile, we noticed that the girl went progressively downhill physically, emotionally and academically. (And we never heard that she won the Nobel Prize either.) Today, that would not happen. Proper dress is sometimes negotiable and while some special needs students do get "reasonable accommodations," even they do not go home and loll around, eating Twinkies. Physical education and exercise is a must for all.

A study by Dr. Linda May and her colleagues at Kansas City University of Medicine and Biosciences indicates that the benefits of exercise accrue even before the baby is born. Exercise by pregnant moms benefits babies as well as the moms. Expectant moms, who did moderate aerobic exercise three times a week, had fetuses with more mature nervous systems, lower heart rates and breathing that was longer and deeper, improving their overall health.

If allowed to explore, babies of course, are veritable moving machines—rolling over, creeping, crawling, pulling up, and walking instinctively, if not inhibited. Responsive cheers always help. The running, chasing, climbing and exploring that young children do as they grow serves to develop growth in several domains. Access to playground equipment, bikes, jump ropes, hula hoops, skates, scooters, skateboards, water toys and floats, trampolines, moon bounces, etc. only add to the well-being of children, and when properly supervised, they elicit brain health and physical fitness.

Some benefits that naturally and almost miraculously accrue through gross motor movement are:

- Eye, ear, hand, foot and body coordination
- Dominance
- Sidedness
- Sensory integration
- Balance
- Proprioception
- Bilateral coordination
- Midline crossing
- Appropriate movement
- Motor planning
- Strength
- Stamina

In addition to these physical benefits, mental benefits are also linked to exercise. And the list of benefits is growing. Reporting on studies at the Salk Institute in California, NY Times science reporter, Gretchen Reynolds shares that exercise increases blood flow in the hippocampus, frontal and prefrontal regions of the brain, thereby stimulating new brain cell growth. This leads to improved memory, executive function, attention span, concentration and psychomotor speed. The oxygen exchange also builds brain cells by increasing energy, stamina, and endurance.

> If there is one "magic bullet for learning" it is exercise, says John Ratey in his book, *Spark*. Exercise, he asserts, can increase academic performance, improve mood, and reduce levels of violence and depression.

In 2010 the National Institutes of Health (NIH) studied many of the products and programs on the market that were making claims to increase cognitive growth. They looked at a great number of foods, vitamins, supplements, gadgets, brain gyms, and practices. "Exercise," was one of the very few confirmed to have positive results. According to science reporter, Sharon Begley, reporting in *Newsweek* Magazine, "Exercise emerges as a clear winner in rejuvenating and preserving cognitive health."

But exercise is not the norm for all children. One third of school children in America are now considered to be obese. The accessibility of junk food, the use of electronics, and the reluctance of parents to encourage their children to go outside and play, all impact fitness. Clearly most kids are not exercising as they should. Parents need to set guidelines, and enforce them to make sure their kids are moving.

Most school districts today offer a variety of athletic opportunities beyond the school day. If they are not convenient in location or on the schedule, parents may want to consider carpooling , trading services—or doing whatever is necessary to get and keep their kids involved in physical activity.

But if organized sports still don't appeal or work for your child or the schedule, consider other options: biking, skating, working out at a gym, doing yoga, Zumba, aerobics, or playing video games that involve whole-body movement, and that have more flexible scheduling. Go hiking with your child on local nature trails, run in the park, or at the local high school track. Again, look for balance in schedules and life-style. If they seem lopsided, brainstorm some ways to bring them back into balance. Sometimes certain activities may need to be eliminated to make room for physical fitness.

Again, don't overlook jobs around the house. Some suitable for older students can be as vigorous as a full aerobic workout: housecleaning, gardening, lawn mowing, and gardening, painting, sweeping, scrubbing, raking, shoveling, chopping wood, car washing, etc. You can decide whether you want to pay for these jobs or chalk it up to family responsibility. That's a personal decision.

Many districts have developed and implemented wellness policies that address nutrition and physical activity. Some have ongoing health councils. Parents can sit on these councils and put their creative ideas to use. Don't be afraid to approach your district, and ask about the existence or their status—or the possibilities of establishing a wellness council with some friends. Offer to lend a hand if you are able. Parents can make a big difference. In my former district, parents helped introduce healthier choices for school lunches and snacks; they changed vending machines for the better; they introduced creative new games at recess and raised funds to purchase new playground equipment; they introduced walking clubs, and led morning yoga exercises. Most principals love their health councils. "They channel parent energy and expertise in a cooperative and meaningful way," one said as he proudly reported out to the school board. Everyone gains. The National Alliance for Nutrition and Activity (NANA) offers assistance.

◆ ◆ ◆

Strategy 7:

Nutrition

What we allow our kids to put in their mouths affects not only their bodies, but their minds and emotions, as well.

Just as knowing your children's interests and natural strengths increases your chances of helping them academically, but knowing their eating habits and preferences is also critical. Eating habits provide clues to how their brains work. What foods do they crave? Which foods make them drowsy or hyper? What foods do they avoid? How do they react to certain foods? There are a small number of children, for example who do better in the morning without breakfast because they process glucose differently, but they are the exception. Most children require a hearty breakfast, or they will simply spend the morning in a brain fog. So observe their habits and reactions and jot your observations down.

Be alert for signs of allergies—even mild ones. According to the U.S. Food and Drug Administration, the eight most common irritants, accounting for more than 90% of food allergies are: milk, eggs, peanuts, tree nuts (such as almonds, cashews, walnuts,) fish, shellfish, soy and wheat. Chronic post-nasal drip, low energy, hyperactivity, stomach disorders, headaches, and of course, hives or skin disorders may be signs of a food allergy. Discuss this issue with your pediatrician if you have concerns.

We are learning more about nutrition every day. Certain foods are higher in nutrients that foster brain power:

- Blueberries, pomegranates, acai berries, and almost all other berries appear to enhance memory. Live foods, living foods—fruits, vegetables, seeds, and beans engender life. Sugar and refined carbohydrates, and caffeine in children lead to fatigue and mood disorders.

- Foods that contain Omega 3 fatty acids, such as walnuts, almonds and fish,—especially salmon, mackerel, sardines, and anchovies (though most kids abhor anchovies)—are believed to build more resilient memories, and stave off depression. Omega 3's as a group are generally considered to be the building blocks of good brains.

- Foods rich in protein, such as yogurt, peanut butter, lean meats and eggs aid in attention and memory.

- Iron rich foods, such as raisins and red meats play a key role in transporting oxygen into the brain, increasing alertness.

- Complex carbohydrates (fruit, vegetables, nuts, seeds and grains) will fuel the brain, maintain a good glycolic index, and help stabilize concentration. They will assist the brain in running steadily at peak performance.

- Cruciferous vegetables—broccoli, cauliflower, and Brussels sprouts—are all rich in choline, another essential nutrient for memory and brain health. Choline is a precursor to the neurotransmitter acetylcholine, which contributes to healthy and efficient brain processes.

- Cinnamon is known to increase reaction time.

(Also, many vitamins such as the B's and D's and supplements such as ginko, vinpocetine, acetyl carnetine, etc. have been reputed to give a mental boost in adults, particularly in memory, but have not been studied in children).

For too long the public has not paid particular attention to what they put into their bodies—which of course, also affects the mind, emotions and spirit.

The list of harmful ingredients—herbicides, pesticides, hormones and the like which have seeped into our food chain, has grown exponentially. Organic foods, while increasing in availability, are still not fully understood nor priced attractively to fit into many budgets, but are usually preferable. Some simple things almost anyone can do to take advantage of better nutrition are:

- Involve children in planning menus.
- Involve them in shopping for healthy foods.
- Encourage them to help prepare simple dishes with you.
- Allow them to pack their own lunches.

- Consider a garden. If you do not have room for a plot outdoors, consider an indoor garden. Gardens in pots or bags that grow plants vertically are viable anywhere.
- Surf the internet with your children for some attractive healthy recipes to hook their interest.
- Serve meals around the same time every day, because kids respond well to routines. Don't allow snacks or drinks within one hour of mealtime.
- Don't force children to clean their plates. This could actually traumatize the child and set them up for problems later in life.
- Check out the new guidelines recommended by the United States Department of Agriculture (USDA) online.

The internet is a great source of ideas for getting kids to eat vegetables—such as encouraging kids to dip small carrots, celery sticks or broccoli pieces into yogurt, ranch dressing, applesauce, or hummus. Variations on pizzas can be made very nutritious, as can many varieties of muffins—both encompassing a variety of veggies. Jessica Seinfeld's book, *Deceptively Delicious*, has many excellent tips for fussy eaters, including recipes for pureeing cauliflower and other vegetables so they can be "slipped" into their favorite dishes, such as macaroni and cheese, without any taste difference.

Michele Obama has done a great job encouraging schools to get involved in wellness, including better nutrition. Her book, *American Grown: The Story of the White House Kitchen Garden and Gardens Across America*, has fine ideas for encouraging parents and children to grow their own food.

Be vigilant regarding curriculum at your child's school. Make sure that school boards do not cut or shorten health and physical education courses, (where nutrition is often discussed). Again, ask about the status of a school health council in your district or school, and consider starting one with a friend, if none exists. Don't be shy about approaching administration. Remember, the schools belong to you!

♦ ♦ ♦

Strategy 8:

Sleep

Sleep is finally starting to give up some of its secrets.
Now we just have to follow along.

Not long ago *Time Magazine* covered a story about the South Korean police raiding a late night hangout. Teenagers were rounded up by the dozens. Their parents were fined. No, they were not drinking or dancing, nor even doping. They were studying—cramming for their upcoming tests, but doing so past the permissible hour. According to the South Koreans, students should be home in bed sleeping, instead of burning the midnight oil to get better grades on their tests. Their law mandates a strict curfew, but those kids were up past that appointed curfew hour, and the teachers were in collusion. "GOTCHA!" the police announced, shining their flashlights in the faces of the culprits, causing them to scramble like uncovered insects. "You're all under arrest. So when both teachers and students were cuffed, taken downtown and slapped with a hefty fine, the world was shocked. "No one can say the South Koreans don't appreciate the value of a good night's sleep," one reporter quipped, "and maybe, that's partially why South Korea ranks second in the world in math and science scores (compared with America's paltry 17th and 21st place rankings).

But it's hard to convince teenagers they need more sleep. They are a tough group to crack. Not only are they often sleep deprived, but their biological clocks seem to have idiosyncrasies. Some studies suggest that during adolescence, clocks shift forward, compelling teens to stay up late, and sleep way past the normal start of school in traditional settings. A few districts have wisely taken this into account, and modified their starting and ending times. If yours is one of them, support that move, or if not, you may want to encourage administration and your school board to explore it.

Even most adults don't realize that the brain during sleep consumes twenty times the energy as it does during thinking; and that during sleep the brain is working very hard to get ready to do more work. Dr. Avaro Pascual-Leone shared new findings regarding the pivotal importance of sleep at a recent international forum. "Sleep is not the background to the symphony," he said. "It IS the symphony. The brain at rest is not at rest." During sleep our brains consolidate or make permanent what we've learned. Some experts even suggest taking a nap right after we've learned something new to retain that content.

Psychologist William Killgore of Harvard Medical School says, "Sleep clears out the cognitive underbrush—a little like running a clean-and repair program on your biological hard drive."

Studies show that lack of sleep is related to ADHD, childhood obesity, childhood depression, and poor grades. McKenna (2007) goes so far as to assert that the effects of sleep loss are "akin to lead exposure."

But how do we get our kids to buy in? So many still secretly read books under the covers with flashlights, and have now added iPads, Kindles, cell phones, online videogames and other devices to their secret caches, making this a worse condition than reading the books. The light from the screen tricks the brain into thinking that it's daytime, disrupting one's biorhythms. So take a leaf from the South Korean police. Rout them out. Insist that they get a good night's sleep. Enforce that law.

According to Matthew MacDonald's work, *Your Brain: The Missing Manual*, the recommended sleep requirements for children and adults are:

Age	Average Hours of Recommended Sleep/Day
Newborn	18
1 month	5-16
3 months	15
6 months	14-15
9 months	14
1 year	13-14
2 years	13
3 years	12
4 years	11-1/2
5 years	11
6 years	11
7 years	10
8 years	10
9 years	9-10
10–17 years	9-11
Adults	7-8
Elderly	7-8

Chances are your kids (and you) are probably not getting the required sleep. Almost nobody does on a regular basis. We are a nation of sleep-deprived persons, and many don't realize it.

Knowing what we now know about sleep and its influence on our brain functioning as well as overall health, proper sleep should be near the top of our "to do" lists.

Some aides to a better sleep are:

- A consistent sleep routine—sticking to the same bedtime, and the same tasks or rituals before going to bed
- Establishing rules about the use of technology (none after a certain hour; phones turned off; or phones left in the kitchen or parent's bedroom; no reading under the covers)
- A room that is cool and dark
- A comfortable mattress
- Quiet stress free surroundings that are conducive to relaxation
- Minimal noise
- No exercise late at night
- Bedrooms a distance from any TV
- Minimal light intrusion
- No caffeine drinks at least two hours before bedtime

Examine your and your children's habits. This is one area that parents may have to look to themselves and the example they are setting.

Really competitive kids may have trouble believing this new research, so parents may also need to open their eyes by sharing some of the research.

Failing to get enough sleep can also cut off an important source of creativity: our dreams. Until recently, the significance of our dreams was concealed from all of us. But now fMRIs, PET scans, and high density EEGs—can watch the nocturnal brain at work. They can see how it ticks throughout the sleep cycle. And to the surprise and delight of researchers, this is shedding light on that most elusive of phenomenon: creativity. Harvard University psychologist Deidre Barrett, tells us that during sleep, the brain is thinking much more visually and intuitively."

Barrett has conducted studies that suggest that engaging in some type of pre-bedtime priming—contemplating a problem you'd like to solve, for example—then falling asleep and letting the mind do its work, may solve the problem for you. Up to a third of the subjects in her sample group reported that priming had helped them find a solution that had eluded them during the day.

We've all slept on a problem and had it sort itself out by the morning. Even Albert Einstein who slept ten hours a night used pre-bedtime priming to help solve his toughest problems and recommended it to others. (Let your teenagers know that one, too.) Sleep can be a source of good ideas, and it's exciting that we're finally learning how to dip into some of these.

◆ ◆ ◆

Strategy 9:

Plasticity: Our Adaptable Bodies and Brains

Most students sense they have the seeds of greatness within them. They just don't always know how to bring them out.

Parents can help their children gain awareness of their physical powers and adaptability.

- Read or use a search engine to brush up on "plasticity" and how the body and brain can change.
- Then share this with your child. Teach him some basic facts about the human body and the human brain's dynamics. Emphasize its plastic nature.
- Be playful—use rubber bands, silly putty or Playdoh to get the points across—especially that the body and

brain are flexible and will respond to your will and its environment. Teach them that "The mind is a muscle. If you use it, it will grow."

- Press a key or a coin into come clay or playdoh to show how easily impressions can be made. So it is with our brains.

- Use metaphors such as Plastic Man or Gumby to demonstrate flexibility. Our brains are a bit like them, with "superpowers" waiting to be brought out.

- When we work our bodies and brains hard, they grow. So stretch them.

- Show them before-and-after pictures of bodies and brains that have had a healthy workout.

- Ask the child to visualize the brain socializing in its neighborhood—chattering and exciting its neighbors—firing off new neurons—making new friends and forming new connections and friendships. This encourages the "neighborhood" to grow. Can you picture this expansion? Describe it.

- Assure them that they are in "charge of a lot." Teach them that challenging activities can be the most fun, and that even our mistakes help us learn and grow. Sometimes our failures are our finest lessons."

Chapter 5:
The Affective Domain

INTRODUCTION:

The affective realm takes in the social and emotional aspects of an individual, and is one of the most elusive to understand. Despite this, it's to our advantage to try to comprehend it, because more and more we are discovering the affective realm wields great power.

In fact, it is now believed that all major decisions are made at the feeling level. For example, if a child, even a baby, decides to explore, it's only in part because physiology drives them to do so. Overriding that, are the child's feelings, which tell them it is okay. The same applies to most of our actions—children's and adult's.

In 2001, Daniel Goleman brought some of this to our attention in his landmark book *Emotional Intelligence*. He underscored the role of affect in learning and in modifying behavior. He asserted that emotional intelligence (EQ) dwarfed intellectual intelligence (IQ,) and also pointed out that much academic underachievement was linked to deficits in the affective realm. Research in the intervening years has only strengthened Goleman's position, and supports the fact that emotions are the triggering mechanisms for higher cognitive functions.

The mind takes in twenty million pieces of information per minute, but processes only a small fraction of those. The affective realm works like powerful software running in the background-filtering and prioritizing what it believes to be most important. It will then push to the forefront those pieces of information (among the twenty million taken in) that are deemed most relevant. That is power!

We see this play out often. A student with a headache won't be concentrating on much else. And we wouldn't expect that student to learn much in that condition, would we? So it is, that a social or emotional distraction, such as difficulties with a boyfriend or girlfriend, or thoughts about a squabble on the school bus, will take precedence over learning content. We can never fully understand what a child is thinking when she isn't attending to her academics, but should generally suspect something in the affective realm.

Until now, we've focused on the knowledge revolution that has mostly pertained to neuroscience, genomics and in the physical realm, the need for certain nutrients, exercise and sleep. But much has also been revealed in the other domains, too. In his 2011 book, *The Social Animal*, author David Brooks sheds light on some of the new knowledge in the affective realm, and how our bodies and brains work together to interface with our emotions..

According to Brooks, we now know that:

- "Much, if not most of the impressive action is happening at the unconscious level, below our level of awareness." (As an example of this, Nobel Laureate, Eric Kandel explained that when we speak, 75–80 % of what we say is governed by content at the unconscious level, such as rules of grammar, etc. Our conscious minds are controlling only a small amount of our thoughts at any given point.)
- "Our unconscious minds shape our character, our integrity, our biases and our intelligence."
- "For a long time, we have viewed reason as being over here, and emotion over there, and the two have been at war with each other. The assumption has been that if you're emotional, you're not rational, and if you're rational, you're not emotional."

- "Emotions are not the enemy of thinking. Emotions are at the center of thinking. They are the foundation of reason."
- "Finally, the disciplines are starting to come together, and we're experiencing some sort of truce and synergy of understanding."

Brooks goes on to say that "More and more people are beginning to appreciate the impact of the internal self. They ask:

- What's inside?
- What powers do we hold?
- What should we do with these powers?
- What are our limits?
- Can we change them? If so, how?
- What do our neuropathways have to do with changes?
- How can we raise our children to be happy individuals who relate well to others and lead good lives?"

Such issues take up more of our time and thought than we ever realized, and should be taken into consideration. Brooks asserts that three fundamental factors correspond to how successful and fulfilling our lives will be:

1. How well we relate to people
2. How well we understand situations
3. How well we perceive the world

It's good to know what's on our children's minds and what they'll need to know to succeed in the future. But these are not the kinds of things ordinarily taught in schools. We would do well to consider our own responses and reactions and bear them in mind as we shepherd our children and point them toward success in life through balanced lifestyles.

♦ ♦ ♦

Strategy 10:

Bonding—Responsiveness and Reciprocity

Grace Kelly and Bing Crosby used to sing a little song: "I give to you and you give to me. True Love. True Love."
That's spells reciprocity—a critical element in raising baby, and maintaining relationships through life.

In discussing physical bonding, we pointed out that almost nothing is ever purely just "physical," or just, "affective," etc. Most responses cross over and encompass some of the affective, cognitive and transcendent as well. The same can be said of the affective dimensions of bonding— that experience of getting to know one's baby. It's an integrated experience, and a truly formidable one in its own right. Bonding, overall, is one of life's peak experiences—the closest thing to falling in love. Those early months, in particular, are intense. A parent once described his take on bonding:

"It's Romeo and Juliet.

Bogey and Bacall.

Antony and Cleopatra.

All the classics and so much more

All rolled into one."

The "falling in love" analogy makes sense. Consider the similarities involved beyond the pure physical:

- Ongoing and careful observation
- Attunement to each other's mood with appropriate responses

- Listening
- Eye Contact
- Mirrored feelings
- Empathy
- Language
- Negotiating
- Reaching out in tender touches
- Gleeful sharing
- Lots of verbal and non-verbal communication
- Shared experiences and moods
- Harmony
- A sense of being as one
- Release of oxytocin and prolactin
- Overall responsiveness and reciprocity

The last two—responsiveness and reciprocity—have recently been isolated as particularly dynamic and more important to the young baby than almost anything else—even, more so than language stimulation, which has long been seen as the intellectual Holy Grail.

> Few deny the critical importance of language stimulation! But in fact, according to new findings, responsiveness and reciprocity trump this, and almost all other affective and cognitive priming gestures.

Self-worth and cognitive readiness both grow out of responsiveness and reciprocity.

So what do responsiveness and reciprocity look like in the young baby? There is no formula, of course, but here are some examples:

Baby squints. Mom or Dad mimic baby's action. They squint too.

Baby chortles. Mom and Dad chuckle back.

Baby cries out for food. Mom or Dad responds with the breast or a bottle.

Baby wets and is uncomfortable. The parents come to the rescue. They respond—all very ordinary gestures, but apparently packed with power.

As children grow, of course, responsiveness and reciprocity take different forms, but hopefully you get the idea. In all our relationships we look for and respond to the positive reactions of those close to us. In fact, we thrive on them.

Whenever parents quickly respond to baby's needs, he is affirmed. He interprets it as, " I love you. You, Baby, are the Center of the Universe—a magnificent being, close to my heart." This fills him up with love. It helps him develop confidence. It sets the stage for future growth and is directly related to how well baby learns now and will learn in the future. Baby's needs should come first whenever possible—especially in the first few months.

Without a doubt, though, language acquisition is important business—key to social, emotional and academic success. NYU researchers Catherine Tamis LeMonk and Marc Bornstein, have long studied this in babies and young children. These experts now conclude that "one of the mechanisms helping a baby to talk, isn't parents' speech at all… it's what the parent accomplishes with a well-timed loving caress or touch or eye contact. It's the timing of it all. It's the _**responsiveness**_ to what the baby initiates that matters the most."

They go on to concur that while quantity of language is important, it now appears that it's even more important to RESPOND—to the child-- to pick up what's coming FROM the baby, and react to that.

Babies and toddlers need real live humans to see them and to hear them and to give them feedback. They depend on this and require this to help them grow and develop. That's why TV and DVD's don't work well. They do not react to the baby's signals—that dense tangle of rich and complicated communication that's coming from the baby's eyes, mouth, and hands. Elmo and Dora, for example, are adorable, but they cannot interact. They cannot pick up a child's cues. Nor can Baby Einstein respond to your child's signals. That's where parents and caregivers must come in. That's their job. That's what babies seek and depend on. That's what they need a lot of: reciprocity and responsiveness from a living breathing human—in 4D.

Remember that children, as with all of us, develop only as our environment demands it. So:

- Follow the child's lead.
- Look for cues coming from the baby.
- Concentrate on figuring out what the baby seems to be looking at or stretching to reach. What is exciting him? What is he trying to swat or kick or wave to?
- When you figure it out, then respond immediately.
- But be alert to signs of fatigue. Don't over-stimulate either.

Research shows that babies of mothers who rapidly respond—especially to baby's vocalization—learn to speak earlier and better. One study showed that mothers who were quick to respond to their babies had tots who were six months ahead of "slow responding moms" by age 15 months.

It doesn't have to be complicated. Just chat with Baby. "Okay. I see. You want to touch that zebra swinging from your mobile? Go on." (Mom hits it.) "Now you try. Yes, that's it. It's a zebra. See him swing." Baby touches it with his finger tips. She hugs him and makes eye contact. "Yes. You touched the zebra. Let's try again." Baby is reinforced. He feels the excitement, the love, the power. He's growing in language and inside.

Reciprocity—is a specific type of responsiveness. It involves turn-taking—a back and forth action—some mimicking of what the baby is doing. This, too, helps babies make more sophisticated sounds. "You want to give me the rattle? Thank you. Now it's your turn."

Underlying subtleties can make a huge difference--the timing, the eye contact, the touch, the hugs, the smiles, the sense of fun— all those underlying nuances help. Again, there is no formula. Just tango a bit. Do some double Dutch and juggle as best you can. Welcoming a new baby into the house is always a demanding and time-consuming stage in life, but studying the baby and responding to him will pay off later.

We've focused on the small child here, of course, but don't worry if you feel you've overlooked those early opportunities. There are still plenty ahead. Reciprocity and responsiveness works with older children as well. In fact, it serves us well in all relationships and all stages of life. Taking turns, providing eye contact, give and take in conversation, the timing of one's response—the touch that accompanies recognition—all these continue to be important in our relationships with our children of any age. Just because the research has been done with babies, doesn't mean we can't take away some of this powerful phenomenon. Feel free to extrapolate. Be as sensitive as possible to signals others send you—both verbal and non-verbal. Respond and reciprocate whenever you can. This will pay back in spades.

◆ ◆ ◆

Strategy 11:

"Relaxed Alertness"

Certain moods draw out a child and evoke effort.
"Relaxed alertness" is one of them.

"Relaxed Alertness" is a mood similar to what some call "active listening," and can be very motivating to children and adults alike. I was first introduced to this concept by parents.

- The listener (say, the parent) is receptive and open as the child speaks.

- The parent's eyes are wide and focused on the speaker (the child).

- The listener's body is relaxed. The head nods when appropriate. The tone of voice is agreeable and the timing of response is perfect.

- Without speaking words, the listener says, "I hear you. I'm listening. I'm fully present for you—not rushed. Let's talk. There's nothing more I'd like to do at this moment than hear what you have to say."

Relaxed alertness is an ideal state for receptive learning. It will draw out a child's natural energy. Psychologists Renata and Michael Caine coined the term "relaxed alertness," in the 1990's—and this mode rose to the top of some parent's "to do" lists.

"So you think you have some good ideas for your next birthday party? Really? Let's hear. Uh huh… Sounds exciting… Tell me more." Often the floodgates will open. Both speaker and listener will be in tune and engaged. Effective teachers and guidance counselors will do this naturally. Try to recall one of your favorite teachers or counselors. Chances are they mastered "relaxed alertness." You'd never know the piles of work they had back on their desk. They'd look you in the eye, nod their head, smile and you'd feel like you were the only person in the world at that moment. They had all day for you—just you. Some successful politicians learn to hone this to a high gloss, too. (Some contend that President Clinton largely built his career on this skill.)

Now recall one of your "worst teachers." Odds are, they were either detached and disinterested or totally overbearing or tone deaf to your needs—the sort of parent we do not want to be. Practice "relaxed alertness." It can elicit energy and that bonus—added effort.

◆　◆　◆

Strategy 12:

Study Your Child. Identify His Strengths

My neighbors called me a child worshiper, but I didn't care... The more you know about your baby, the better you can meet her needs.

Learning to be responsive and reciprocal implies a lot of time observing baby, or even an older child. With the baby, especially, it's a frequently recommended practice. "I studied him a lot," one mother said. "I began to learn his rhythms and his preferences—his favorite activities—when he wanted to play, when he didn't want to play, etc. I learned how much play was too much—how much wasn't enough. I began to know when he needed a rest, when he wanted to eat, when he wanted to nap. I gradually learned his preferred sights, smells, sounds, and favorite toys. And I took notes. Some friends criticized me. 'Over the top,' one said. But I didn't care. I was learning so much. I had read that this was a good thing to do, and I agreed. 'Child Worshiper,' another mocked. Similarly, I turned a deaf ear. I felt that the more I knew about my baby, the better I could meet her needs. We were growing in love, and we were both having fun. I still say that it was the right thing to do."

"There's a lot of instinct involved in those early months and years," another parent shared. "You ask a lot of questions, and you learn a lot: How can I make her laugh? (Play peek a boo under the blanket). What causes her to frown? (Parent frowning). And what draws her out? (Tickling). How far do you go? It's something each has to gauge for oneself. A lot of trial and error will go on, but that's part of the mystique of being a parent."

Most of us discover in our own way that babies are self-propelled little organisms—constantly perceiving, learning, and organizing information. Given a wide array of objects and experiences, they'll send out signals. Some responses will be ho-hum. Most will be a little more interesting maybe. But one or two will be a WOW! You'll know you have a HIT. You'll see it in their eyes and body language. When you find something that really clicks, celebrate it. Feed it. Cheer baby on. You'll be helping those neurons chatter and dance, and assisting those genes to express themselves. Cerebral PHANTASMAGORIA! Baby will feel empowered and you can feel good knowing that accelerated learning has begun. Take notes, if you wish, for these are significant moments—as well as important pillars of the learning process. You'll want to build on some of this knowledge now and some in the future.

> With attention and encouragement, the child will dig deeper into his own learning and take charge of his own advancement. That's how significant learning begins. He'll repeat enjoyable experiences.

He'll babble more words, shake more rattles. And as time goes on, he'll build more Legos or tell more stories or play more drums or throw more balls—as he feels the pleasure of the feedback. With empowerment comes readiness for more play and more learning. Even the youngest child will begin to take charge of his own learning when he senses something is a good fit. He will spiral up in skill and in his activities. This is how learning snowballs. This is how we begin to develop confident joyful learners.

"My oldest was fascinated with light switches," a mother shared. I remember my husband carrying him around the house on his shoulders, switching every light in the house on and off. Later he let the baby do it by himself. He would shriek and squeal with delight and that thrilled us, too. We didn't care about the electric bill. We knew it was more important that he be thrilled to the core—and also learn this cause and effect relationship. To this day, he's fascinated by all things electronic. There's no question where he's going in his career." She went on. "My younger daughter also loved high drama, too. But she specialized in banging on pots and pans and singing along for what seemed like hours at a time. We bought her a drum set for her second birthday. Then later, we let her graduate to karaoke, then to the piano. She performs solos in all the school concerts. We're proud of her. And we trace her skills to those early years."

◆　◆　◆

Strategy 13:

Learn Your Child's Interests

Back in the 1940's and early 1950's there was very popular radio show called: "The Quiz Kids." It was a quiz bowl format, and showcased some of the smartest kids in the country, who would compete for war bonds by answering questions on a variety of topics. Producers of the show combed the nation for these little prodigies, and the show ran for about twelve years. Over this time, the "regulars" became enormously popular, receiving hundreds of requests for personal appearances, and thousands of fan letters every week. At one point they were ushered around Hollywood, appearing with top celebrities, such as Bing Crosby, Bob Hope and Eddie Cantor. Eventually the show left the air, but many years later, one of the original Quiz Kids, Ruth Duskin Feldman, tracked down and interviewed many of the regulars—her former "colleagues," to see how life had treated them. As expected, results varied, but one conclusion she shared at a conference was that the Quiz Kids who had identified a strong interest early on in life and vigorously pursued clear goals, fared better than those equally talented individuals, who did not. All the Quiz Kids were "generalists"—possessing a broad fund of general knowledge or they would not have made it through the auditions. But some also went on to specialize in some narrow field, (such as engineering, math, or television production.) And those tended to be happiest with their work trajectories and their lives, in general—definitely more so, than those who remained generalists and did not specialize in a particular field or career. The former quiz kids who remained generalists, typically had a more checkered career profile, lower earnings, and less overall life satisfaction. Their life trajectories were more fragmented. The message shared by many of the former Quiz Kids was that while it helps to be well-rounded, with a deep fund of general knowledge, there is no substitute for depth in some specialty.

It may help if parents begin early on to study the baby—ferreting out his temperament, his likes and dislikes, his intense interests, and his lags, guiding him along a fitting and friendly path, and encouraging as much positive feedback as possible in areas of interests.

Day One in a baby's life is not too soon to take in and record some of the nuances. Is he calm? Energetic? Alert in the evening or the morning hours? What are his favorite activities? Preferred sights, smells and sounds? Does he prefer animals? People? Gadgets? What types? Noise? Silence? Music? What are his favorite toys? How would you describe his temperament?

Jot down simple observations: "Today he nearly jumped out of his infant seat at the sight of my sister's dog," or "She went wild for Uncle Bob's Hip Hop music—shaking her head from side to side, and rocking out as best an eight month old can do" or "He was frightened by the sudden appearance of some ants on the picnic blanket. He panicked and started to wail" or "Gave a deep belly laugh at the baker's funny faces!"

Be a detective. Over time you'll see patterns emerge and these will be clues to your child's inner life—possibly even signs of where his future may lie. Don't fret over lags (all babies have some). It's the strengths that matter the most. Above all, you will always want to build on those strengths. This will help direct your purchases and decisions—the toys, books, later magazines, games, and software you'll buy and the enrichment courses or summer camps he'll attend.

Buy a nice book early on to keep track of your notes. Leather ones and nubby tweeds work well. They hold up, and you'll want to keep this for the long haul. But a plain marble copybook can work well, too. Notes can be simple or complex—short or long.

Consider purchasing a keepsake box to go along with the book. This gives you a central place to store report cards, programs, awards, etc., and over time will also help you track trends and provide a "data base" to draw from in the future. (Sometimes a preteen or teen is confused about which courses to elect, or direction to pursue, for example. And you can then "mine the data" for early signs of proclivities and interests.) Or you may just want to share your journal notes with your child. Kids love to hear about themselves, and they'll be flattered that you took the time to do this.

Learning Styles

Another useful pattern for tracking the way your child takes in the world is by noting his learning styles. It helps to know if she is primarily a visual, auditory or kinesthetic learner. All humans have a preferred way of processing information and knowing this can help accelerate learning. Some parents pick this up naturally and are even unaware that they are doing so. Others are more systematic in their attention to learning styles.

Visual: You'll know you have a visual baby, for example, if he's extremely attracted to vivid colors, bright pictures and will concentrate on an image for an extended period of time. Visual babies will easily make eye contact and will appear fascinated by dangling objects.

Auditory babies are easily entertained by language, sound, and familiar voices. They love music. They are early talkers and hyper-sensitive to noise. The mall or sporting events are not their favorite places, as they can easily go on overload and be upset by them.

Kinesthetic babies wiggle and squirm a lot. They creep, crawl, climb and walk early. It's hard to keep these babies down. They love hands-on activities and manipulative toys. Keep the knickknacks out of view. And get ready to roughhouse and play a lot of ball if you have a kinesthetic baby.

Again, jot your observations and conclusions down. Make it part of the running record that you've begun. Like the rest of your notes, these can act as a touchstone when you want to go back and review the child's whole profile.

Most children will prove to be combination learners. But most also show one preference, and this can be useful information to help hasten learning. This is how you can put learning styles to use:

Suppose you want to teach your preschooler how to throw a ball. You've taken notes and teased out that he's a visual, auditory, kinesthetic learner in that order. Use this information to teach him how to throw a ball more efficiently. Follow these steps:

1. First use a visual approach (since this is his dominant learning mode). Show him how to throw. Slowly demonstrate the steps several times. Let him <u>SEE</u> how to throw. He should be most attentive.

2. Next, describe the steps as you repeat them. He is <u>HEARING</u> now—his second best bet to catch on is auditory.

3. Lastly, practice in slow motion how to throw the ball. Demonstrate, and now have him <u>PRACTICE</u> what he's seen and heard. This is a kinesthetic approach.

By appealing to his preferred modes in the right order, there will be less frustration and quicker learning.

Tracking kids' interests and proclivities is informative. Learning can made to be more fun. Bonding is easier. Kids can be set on a productive course at an earlier age.

◆　◆　◆

Strategy 14:

Unconditional Love

Unconditional love is difficult to attain, but remains the worthiest of goals.

Lucky is the child whose parents have taken the time to ask a few questions of their own before children came along: "Who are we? Where are we going? What values do we share? Do we want children? If so, what kind of life do we want to carve out for ourselves and for them?"

And luckier still, is the child whose parents have agreed on a credo, and present a united front. This helps the parents go forward in parenthood, free to confer unconditional love on each other and on the child. This is the best possible scenario for any parent and child.

Unconditional love is what makes the world go around—the most powerful force in the universe. It is the greatest gift one can give—worthy of whatever pains are necessary to attain it. It says to another, "No matter what happens in your life, whatever struggles or pains you may face, I will always be there for you. You are mine, and I am yours. And you can always count on me. Nothing you could do could change that." It is what we should all seek to confer on our children. It is what we all seek in our own lives.

Famed anthropologist, Ashley Montagu had this to say of unconditional love: "From this central sun, all virtues flow, all potentialities are maximized. It is the most perfect of all the conservers of mental and physical health, the highest form of intelligence, and the most effective of disciplines… And love grows the love of learning."

This kind of love fills up a person—especially a child. That child not only learns better, but he feels more secure and confident. He will face the world openly and with enthusiasm, ready to soak up all the opportunities life has to offer. Unconditional love also protects one from assaults. It serves as a Lucite shield in times of trial.

One of the best examples I've ever witnessed involved an eighth grade girl, caught in an unfortunate situation. She was a little shy and seemingly unsure of herself—as so many at that age are. But she was a good student and from a fine family, which conferred a secret resiliency that I would come to notice. Some of her tentativeness, though, showed through at school on a particular day. A notorious bully honed in on her as she passed him with her cafeteria tray.

"Hey you," he called.

"Huh?... me?" she said.

"Yea, you... You with the hair on your head." His clique at the table laughed out loud. "Ha. Ha. Ha," This just egged him on. "I'm sorry, girlie. I meant to say, 'You with the strings hanging down from your skirt.' (More Ha Ha. Ha's.)—all out of earshot of the administrator. The girl looked down.

"Uh oh. Those aren't strings at all," he mocked. "Excuse me. They're legs, aren't they? Ha. Ha. Ha. Ha. My mistake. Ha. Ha. Ha. Ha. Ha." The followers whistled and jeered, pointing to the young girl's pathetically thin, undeveloped legs.

"Let's see how strong they are... " the ringleader challenged, leaning forward and tripping the rattled girl, who went down with a thud, food clattering all about. Spaghetti. Meatballs. Chocolate milk. Salad. Flying in every direction. What a mess! And what a disastrous scene for anyone—not to mention a sensitive pre-teen.

Suddenly an administrator appeared on the scene, ushering the bully and accomplices into the office, and enlisting help so the girl could get cleaned up. When I discussed it later with a counselor, we both suspected and feared this could scar the girl for life .

But amazingly, this did not seem to be the case. The girl returned to school after that, unapologetic and graceful. Somehow she showed no signs of trauma. When the bullies returned from their suspension, she even stared them down when she passed them again in the cafeteria. They just looked the other way.

Somehow this tender soul managed to take the incident in stride, and bounced back. Others noticed and admired her. Eventually she rose to a position as leader in her grade.

The guidance counselor and I marveled. We wondered how she could rebound like that, and concluded that it was partially because she came from such a warm and loving family that offered acceptance and unconditional love. That love bolstered her and prepared her for life's trials. Beneath the fragile facade, she obviously had a steely core. Yes, she was momentarily hurt. But the damage was limited, and one sensed that inside she knew she was worthy. Others without those internal resources would not have. That's what unconditional love can do for a child.

A lot goes on during those school years that students never share with their parents. And some of it is not pretty.

> But when those ugly moments come—and they will come to all at some point in different degrees, one hopes their child will be able to cope. This is more apt to occur if they are wrapped in the cocoon of your unconditional love.

What can parents do to foster this?

- Stay close with your child.
- Communicate regularly.
- Express your love physically and verbally.
- Let him know that he can share anything with you.
- Let him know that he is the most important thing in the world to you, and nothing can ever change that.
- Listen to him when he talks to you. Touch him to affirm your love.
- Look at him with soft eyes.

Oprah Winfrey was once asked how she managed to stay so successful as an interviewer for so long. She drew upon some wisdom shared by her friend, the author, Toni Morrison. Oprah said: "Everybody just wants to be heard... What every child wants to know is, Do your eyes light up when I enter the room? Did you hear me and did what I say mean anything to you? That's all they're all looking for." (And that was about as cogent a description of unconditional love as I've ever heard.) Think about it. Do your eyes light up when they come into the room?

Beware of telling children that you love them for their grades, or prizes or awards or for work they do around the house or for a gift or card they have made. In so doing, you inadvertently communicate that love is something given in return for something else. True love, however, is given unconditionally because of who you are, not because of what you do or what you achieve.

And when they stray (and they all will at times,) remind them that you love them, but you do not love the choices that they have made. Separate the person from the action. They will have to accept the consequences of their acts, but that does not mean you love them any less. Assure them that nothing they could ever do could make you love them less.

Someone one asked at a meeting how a parent can determine if you give enough love, and a participant referred him to the Bible: (Corinthians 13:4–8). This is the passage so often recited at weddings. It may help to measure oneself against those attributes:

Love is patient.

Love is kind.

Love does not envy.

Love does not boast.

Love is not proud.

Love does not dishonor others.

96

Love is not self-seeking.

Love is not easily angered.

But love always protects, trusts, hopes and perseveres.

Count up your responses. This will give you a pretty good idea of how well you confer unconditional love in your life.

◆ ◆ ◆

Strategy 15:

Praise

Most parents think praise is always a good thing to do.
But sometimes praise can hurt more than it helps.

Who hasn't used praise to encourage their kids to work harder? It seems like such a logical way to encourage students to keep striving, doesn't it? But psychologist, Carol Dweck, has concerns. She says that many of us don't use praise in the right way, or use too much of it. Praise, she says, can sometimes do more harm than good. First, she's concerned that American parents confuse lavish praise with raising self-esteem—a notion that has been disproved. Second, she is convinced that American parents praise their children in the wrong ways. They use vague phrases such as "you're so smart" or "It seems that you can do anything," but are not specific enough about their actions. This can actually harm children.

In one experiment, Dweck showed that students who were told they were smart actually tried *less* hard on a subsequent task. (Presumably they were anxious to hold on to that smart label, and became fearful of taking future risks. "Why jeopardize my reputation as a smart kid? I won't take a chance.") What those students didn't know, was that by curtailing intellectual risks, they were almost surely limiting their own intellectual growth.

In this same study, students who were *not* told they were smart, but rather praised for their *"effort,"* continued to work very hard. ("I'm proud of you for working so hard on that assignment," etc.) And the next time those kids had a choice to select a new task, (hard or easy) most opted for the hard one. They weren't afraid of taking risks and wanted to grow. (We can assume that by stretching themselves, those students learned more.) It's important not to praise children too much, and to be specific in the praise you offer. Instead of saying "You're so smart or great," let them know you're proud of their hard work and focus. And be specific. Say, "I like the way you check your work when you're finished an assignment;" or "I like the way you're holding your pencil," or "I like to see you concentrating on your footwork, or free throws"—or whatever seems worthy of note at the time. Don't let vague, profuse, and non-specific praise sidetrack your student and impede future effort. Also, discourage use of labels, such as "smart," "dumb," and so on, altogether if you can. They convey intelligence as a fixed entity, which it is not. Those labels can distort the dynamics of honest praise.

◆ ◆ ◆

Strategy 16:

Listen

My mother used to say, "God gave us two ears, but only one tongue. That tells me He wants us to listen twice as much as we talk."

Listen more. Talk less. Good advice for anybody—especially those who strive to be effective parents—even more so in this hurried frenetic age. Do you recognize yourself in this scenario?

Mom or Dad, whoever gets home first, walks in the door and drops their bags. At first sight of the child, the questions begin to fly fast and furiously:

- What happened in school today? (No answer, but no pause by parent either.) The questions just keep flying:
- What do you have for homework?
- How'd you do on your spelling test?
- Any new assignments?
- Did you eat all your lunch or did you throw your fruit away—again?
- Who did you eat with?
- Have you practiced your piano, etc., etc., etc.

Sometimes while this is going on, the parent is simultaneously checking for emails, texts, and voice mails, or opening snail mail. (Once I overheard a teenager telling a friend about her mother, "I could tell her anything and she wouldn't hear me. Yesterday I said to her, 'Mrs. Jones, the math teacher, took off all her clothes in class today,' and she just kept on checking her mail and rambling on like she does.")

A better approach for parents would be:

- Put down the phone and turn it off awhile when you enter the home.
- Make eye contact when you walk in the door. In the words of Toni Morrison, let "your eyes light up" when you see them. Give them a sense that this is a high point of your day and you are happy to see them. Now, for awhile, you just want their company. You want to hear

what they have to say. Give them no less than you would a valued client.

- Sometimes, say nothing. Silence can be golden--a very valuable tool. Just wait.

- When he or she starts to talk, assume "relaxed alertness"—open body language and good eye contact. This will draw the child out. Then listen—really listen—with your heart and your head.

- Give the child space when you listen. Don't invade. They'll feel more free to express themselves.

- Don't allow technology to intrude on your precious time with your kids. Develop guidelines for its use. Fight to take some time back if you feel you, yourself, are controlled by the lure of the gadgets.

We live in a fragmented culture with a short attention span, which seems to be growing shorter all the time.

Writer Diana Senechal observes that even "our education policies have been hacking away at listening. In some districts a teacher is not supposed to speak for more than 10 or 15 minutes a time, and students are not supposed to stay silent for long. They turn and talk; they perform tasks; they work in groups, they press buttons on gadgets. They may know how to listen for instructions or information but not how to sink into sounds and words. They do not know how to pick up overtones, refrains, allusions... students need to listen to passages beyond their level to grow and stretch."

Senechal wonders, "Who will dare to teach William Blake's 'Augries of Innocence' out loud or Samuel Taylor Coleridge's 'Kubla Kahn'? Who will take students into Walt Whitman's elusive 'A Riddle Song'? Listening requires us to move beyond what we know, expect, or want... Listening involves a certain surrender... a sign of courtesy... and it places limits on chatter."

Senechal adds, "On a practical level, the loss of listening means the loss of basic comprehension."

Parents can help by insisting that children listen from time to time as they read an inspiring poem, or literary passage or even an editorial from the paper that may seem over their heads, but can then be broken down for understanding. Family meetings lend themselves to such activities.

Another rule of thumb is to try to give each child at least fifteen minutes of your undivided attention daily. Some parents tell me this is easiest to do before bedtime.

"They have different bedtimes. I go to their room, and sit on the edge of their bed. I'm prepared to listen. It's amazing what the older ones will share at the end of the day, when they are winding down... It's easier for me to telegraph a sense of my appreciation and love for them, at that time too, as I've had a chance to unwind."

(Larger families might need to split some quality time in the morning.)

◆ ◆ ◆

Strategy 17:

Passing on Your Values

Values are the essence of whom we are. Empathy and responsibility are two that top many lists, and "talk" and "modeling" are used to pass them along.

Empathy:

The golden rule was engraved on a ruler I had as a child. Each kid in the class got one—I think from a local dairy, whose ad was embossed on the back. We set them right up there at the top of the desk, and fiddled with them when we were bored. And sometimes if a student was a little "unruly" the teacher would point to it, and have him read the inscription on the back out loud: "Do unto others as you would have them do unto you." The teacher would repeat it. "That's right, class. That's the golden rule. Now you repeat it." And we did. I can still hear the whole class in unison repeating those words, which were inevitably followed by a short sermon. It sunk in.

In a rudimentary way, and in retrospect, I think it was an earlier generation's attempt at an anti-bullying curriculum, and I must admit it worked pretty well. The Golden Rule advocates for empathy, and has been used to instill that value for thousands of years and through at least twenty five different religions and countless languages. Plato in the fourth century said, "May I do unto others as I would that they should do unto me." Christianity and Judaism teach, "Love they neighbor as thyself." Islam teaches that "None of you truly believes until he wishes for his brother what he wishes for himself," and Buddhism teaches, "Hurt not others in ways that you would yourself find hurtful." The Golden Rule and empathy are as comprehensive a common value as exists.

Basically, empathy is a new term for that. Empathy encourages us to walk in the shoes of another person and to be sensitive to their feelings and their plight. Most parents rank this as one of the most important values they share with their children. We can't count on schools handing out rulers anymore, so parents may have to remember to find time and opportunities to teach the golden rule to their own children.

"We teach empathy primarily through modeling," said one mother, giving an example. "Yesterday, we stopped at a diner on our way to our 5:00 A.M. swim practice. The weather was nasty, and the roads were treacherous, so we stopped on the highway so I could settle my nerves and warm up with some hot chocolate. The waitress gave us excellent service with a smile. Then I overheard her telling a co-worker that she had to get up at 3:00 A.M. to make her kids' lunches and she was afraid she would be late because it was sleeting and the roads were so bad. When she came with the check, I thanked her profusely for being on the job, and made a big fuss about her friendly service—particularly at that ungodly hour. We left a very generous tip, and I made a point to let the kids know it helps to walk in another's moccasins sometimes.

Then later we stopped for gas and the weather was still brutal—sheets of snow and sleet pelting our car. The attendant, standing out there in the mess, smiled as he patiently pumped gas, then took our card. My youngest rolled down his window and shouted. 'Thanks a lot, Mister. It sure must have been hard to come to work today, and to have to serve people in this weather. We appreciate it...' The attendant smiled and waved. 'Did you see that Mom?' my son said proudly as we pulled away. 'That guy smiled at us, even though I know he must have been freezing to death.' Kids sometimes need modeling to find the good around them."

Responsibility:

There are many ways to model responsibility, but homework comes to mind immediately, because it comes up almost every day in homes where there are school-age kids. Homework is a classic responsibility of every student. Some view it as the scourge of all scourges, while others see it as a legitimate bridge between home and school. Invariably, questions arise: Is it necessary? Is it just a ruse to get parents to help with the teachers' work? Why does so much seem like mindless drivel? Why all the tears? How much homework is too much? How much is too little? A few have introduced "reverse homework," where older kids are assigned major research at home, and class time is devoted mostly to teacher review and student support. But, no matter how you look at it, homework in some form appears to be here to stay. I like it because it not only reinforces the class work, but affords students chances to learn personal responsibility and provides parents with opportunities to teach "responsibility."

Educators offer some tips:

- Students need to own their homework. Parents of young students can do homework WITH the child, but not FOR the child.

- Wean off direct parental involvement by fourth grade.

- Remain aware of projects and how they are being done, and offer guidance, such as the proper use of the internet. (It has become too easy for kids to "Google" and to cut and paste. Students need to be taught that this is plagiarism, unless one cites the sources. Such behavior is not only unethical, it is a meaningless exercise.)

- Assign a time and place to do homework. Older children can make these decisions, but parents should discuss it with them.

- Be sure the homework area is well-lit.

- Be available to answer questions and offer guidance and direction when needed.

- Praise students for efforts and diligence when you see it.

The Boston Public School System offers free online "parent guides" to homework, geared to specific grade levels.

Of course, responsibility is also taught in many other ways, including requiring students to do jobs around the house, and being held accountable: taking out the trash, setting the table, walking the dog, scrubbing vegetables, making beds, and clipping coupons, etc. Even older students with crammed schedules and part time jobs, should be expected to do some chores, and research actually shows that the busier the student and the better the grades, the more chores he completes.

Jobs are separate from chores. "Jobs" are special projects sometimes given to one's older children—such as babysitting, mowing the lawn, shoveling the snow, house painting, etc.— things the parents would ordinarily pay someone else to do. Some very organized families even draw up "specs" and simple contracts, which their children sign, and which help to underscore the importance of the responsibility. Pick your style, but by all means, on some level, hold them accountable.

Anti-elitism:

Elitism is something that touches us all, and all children should know of its dangers.

Elitism is one of the most insidious and destructive elements known to man—causing everything from small slights and hurt feelings to major conflicts, wars, and devastating global catastrophes. It's based on the assumption that "My view is superior to yours." "Your family, or religion, or group, or judgment or code of values is inferior to mine." Elitism can be implied, verbalized, or codified, but when it occurs, it invariably leads to misunderstanding, confusion, and/or pushback—in some form, possibly violence. Schools are not immune from elitism. Educators and parents often struggle with tracking and grouping issues, which are sometimes fraught with elitist accusations. Some see "grouping" as diminishing to some children's self-esteem and conducive to elitism in others. A lot of open dialogue needs to occur, so folks gain awareness of the various facets of the issues: How can we provide appropriate levels of stimulation and challenge for those who are ready, and yet maintain a balance of opportunity, a sense of empathy and a cooperative climate for all? How does one build programs that allow one to test one's mettle and soar, without diminishing one's peers or affecting the sense of a team? The answers are not easy.

Modeling of anti-elitism is ideal. Candid conversations and ongoing dialogues should occur if elitist accusations arise, and one does not want detrimental effects to grow.

"Typical" students and their parents can be helped to understand that it's appropriate for everyone to get what he or she needs. (This is no different than coaching for athletics, music, or any other talent.) If one needs a particular academic challenge, then that should be made available. No one would expect a gifted athlete to be deprived of advanced coaching, nor a disabled child to be deprived of individualized help if that is what was needed to meet their needs. Some grouping with intellectual peers would seem advisable at times. These are complex topics, and need to be continually explored and discussed openly.

In addition to open dialogue, personal style needs to be factored into consideration. Top dogs in any area need to learn that if they are overly puffy and exude a superior air, they will be brought down by their peers.

Some parents use direct teaching:

- Never flaunt success. Never exude an air of superiority. Accept compliments with due humility.
- Prepare students ahead of time with appropriate responses when compliments do come their way: "I've been lucky". "A lot of people helped." "Others have had my back." "I have great teachers—or coaches—or mentors." "I've had to work very hard."

- An attitude of genuine gratitude should also be cultivated. A simple thank you. A level voice. A sincere tone. Each will be appreciated.

- Volunteerism and service to others are also important to model. Get involved yourself and bring the kids along. Or check "Volunteer Jobs for Kids," online at *Ask.com*.

It's often very easy to bypass difficult issues, such as the perception of elitism. But this is a mistake. Its complexities will only fester. Enter into a dialogue, preferably with skilled people present. Nelson Mandela once said, "A different world cannot be built by indifferent people."

♦ ♦ ♦

Strategy 18:

The Social Landscape

***When your kids tell you, "It's a jungle
out there," believe them.***

In any open environment, the goal is survival, and sometimes Mama and Papa Bear are clueless as to what's lurking in the brush. Better they should learn what's happening, and maybe lend a hand.

"Mom, you just don't understand," the ninth grader shrieked. "It's not enough to be smart and athletic. Girls need to have good hair, cool shoes, and the right cell phone. I need a raise. I need you to increase my allowance." Right or wrong about the allowance, the girl probably got one thing right: "Mom" probably didn't understand the pressures of the group. Few parents do. When it comes to the social context, parents may as well be on another planet.

The boys, while often less verbal, are just as subject to its vagaries. If pressed, they too, will acknowledge the importance of the right sneakers, videogames, tee shirts, jeans and phones. Any of these eclipse even the SAT's, ACT's, GPA's or anything else on a given day.

> Social networking, with its meteoric rise, hasn't helped. This is an area where the recent knowledge comes up short. No one can really explain what's going on with social networking as its dynamics change faster than researchers can react.

Nobel Laureate Eric Kandel acknowledges that while there have been a few strides in the social realm, such as the understanding of mirror neurons and visual processing, he and others believe it will be a long time before we fathom the social landscape and where technology is taking us—if ever. In some respects the social chasm is growing. (Kids text others in the same room, instead of talking. What's that all about? And everyone e-mails, so there are less face-to-face encounters than ever.) However, in other ways, the social chasm is closing, which is good news. Experts from the social sciences have begun to talk to their colleagues in the "hard sciences," to try to untangle social complexities. Departments are melding, and in a few disciplines at certain universities, departments have even merged. E.O. Wilson, professor emeritus at Harvard, has managed the incredible feat of bringing sociologists and biologists out of their separate silos into a newly created field called sociobiology. Nicholas A. Christakis, professor of sociology and medicine at Harvard says that in the 21st century, it is the biosocial sciences that hold the key to improving human welfare, though "it could be a long time before these disciplines catch up with the study of other domains."

It makes sense that our understanding of human interaction should lag behind other species. For instance, how do you begin to break down the dynamics of bullying on the playground or school bus? Do you say, "Excuse me, Mr. Bully and Ms. Victim? I see there is some bullying behavior going on here. Would you hold on a minute while we hook you up to this hairnet full of electrical probes? We'd like to study what's *really* taking place in your minds?" No. It's doubtful that this will occur anytime soon. Some human interactions are just too complicated. We'll just have to wait.

But if that ever does happen, it will be a great breakthrough. E.O. Wilson reminds us that the most socially astute creatures are those who are adaptable to the needs of the society and invariably they will inherit the earth. Today, he says those are the ants, the termites and the bees, whose legions and cumulative weight far outnumber any other species on earth, including humans. But humans, by aligning themselves with their various social tribes, are strengthening their profiles, and are more apt to thrive this way. In other words, their increasingly strong social bonds are bolstering humanity, and this bodes well for the future. Who knew that Facebook and other social networking activities could make us biologically stronger. With luck, maybe we'll catch up with the ants and become as efficient!

But, according to Wilson, there's also one little problem— humans lack the ants' solidarity and single-minded focus. Our tribes shift so easily and often, which is our downside. Our bonds are often tentative. It's not uncommon to hear one ask questions such as: "Who will I sit with at lunch? Who will take me to the dance?" "Who will fit in best on our work team?" Those many delicate moments mirror the vigilance and vulnerabilities of a real jungle. So maybe the kids are right. We really don't "understand" the social scenarios. Not very well, anyway.

I recently passed a school group on a field trip in Philadelphia. They were all paired off and chatting happily with their partners as they walked through the historic district sites—with the exception of several stragglers, pulling up the rear. Alone and poker-faced, they were obviously disengaged and socially isolated from the rest of the group—a sad thing to see. Presumably, they would gain little from the field trip. In that setting, the social context trumped all else.

Even the brightest kids, I discovered, need to learn to maneuver on their own at times. "Yo smarty pants. Hey, Nerd… Four eyes… Brainiac… Geek… Uber Geek." Despite the teacher's best efforts at prevention, if you talk to kids at the head of the class, they'll tell you they, too, shoulder their share of barbs. In fact they say it's often lonely at the top of the class. It's not unusual to have one's best friend turn on one if the friend thinks he's been cut out of the running for an award or high honor, which happens. Traversing the social landscape can be a challenge for all kids.

And all kids need warmth—shelter from the social storms— reassurance that they are okay. Here are a few ways that parents can help:

- Stay close to your children. Follow their interests and activities. Involve yourself in one or two of their activities, but give them their own space, too.

- Provide unconditional love. "Whatever happens, I'll always be there for you."

- Engage in open and ongoing communication and conversations.

- Be frank and honest, and they will be, too.

- Set limits—especially with technology. Encourage some socializing, but don't allow excessive socializing—either physical or virtual. It can sap energies and distort one's true focus.

- Stay in touch with their friends. Make your home warm and inviting to them from the earliest years.

- Model hospitality and love.
- Eat as a family at least three or four times a week. Hold family meetings where issues can be aired and analyzed, and solve some problems as a team.
- Network with parents of their friends. Not only will you gain valuable information, you'll model the benefits of a wide social network for your child.

Kids need to know that all relationships have their ups and downs, and snags are inevitable. But mostly, friends are a blessing to be cherished. Teach them to problem solve and work things out. Friendships are an absolute necessity for children as they grow.

From the earliest years, parents should invite the children's friends into their homes. Get to know their parents, too, if you can. Invite more than one guest at certain times. Bring in the whole team or scout troop if it seems right to do. Serve food. Be big-hearted. Open your door and lavish their friends with the same kind of love you lavish on your own children. Let them see a smile on your face. Spread the joy and social graces around. Your own kids are watching. They will follow your lead. "Welcome, Robert. Come sit with us for a moment. How are things? What's new in your life? Tell me all about it." Talk in the kids' language. Show interest in their interests. Embrace their funky ways, if they have some. Be accepting and warm, but don't hover or hang out too long—just long enough to make the point that they are welcome and you are glad that they are here, and would like to know what's going on in their lives. Tango... Do double Dutch... Juggle a bit.

As they grow you want to stay close, but not too close. (Another tango lesson here.) You want them to be independent and self-reliant, but to gradually separate. Psychologist and author, Wendy Mogul gave this advice: As children grow, parents should remain available, interested, and vigilant, but not overly enmeshed in their business. She cited these lines from T.S. Eliot—tantamount to a prayer:

> *"Teach us to care.*
> *... And not to care.*
> *Teach us to be still."*

♦ ♦ ♦

Strategy 19:

Family Dinners

Family dinners provide their own type of safety net.

Family Dinners:

> Studies show that students who eat dinner with the family at least three times a week get better grades, have better language skills, and get into less trouble at school and with the law. The statistics are even better in families who eat together five times a week.

Family dinners build closeness. Civilization gets passed on through dinnertime conversations. According to William Doherty, professor of family social science at the University of Minnesota "Family meals are the strongest factor that we've come across in any activity that families do... It really tops them all as a predictor and contributor of a wide range of positive behavior." Strong families, I have known also underscore this.

When a family dines together:

- Language is expressed and enhanced
- Kids get a chance to discuss their school work and parents can tune in
- Everyone gets to share highlights of their day
- Knowledge of current events expands
- Skills of healthy debate are honed
- Parents can spot social and emotional difficulties before they explode
- Kids are given a voice; they feel valued
- Civilization gets passed down

Some common topics are:

- High and low points of the day (Some call these "thorns and roses".)
- Puzzles, brainteasers, trivia, and jokes
- Movies, TV show, websites and games
- Funny or interesting things that came up in class, or on the bus, or on a field trip
- Bloopers—ours and theirs
- Academics—challenges and triumphs; projects and grades
- Chores
- The food—at school and here on the table (Three cheers for Mom and/or the take-out-service.)

Some families even invent their own activities or traditions. One dad shared his own creation: "Stump the Chump"—simple, but fun. Each family member took a turn asking "the Chump"— the person to his right, a trivia question. If he didn't know the answer, he had to go to the encyclopedia to look it up. (Two points if you knew it; one point if you had to look it up.) Then it was the next person's turn. (Sometimes we didn't keep score. We just went around the dinner table—anyone who knew the answer could call out and earn the two points.) We all learned new facts. As parents, we were stumped a lot by our kids—especially in the science department, but we learned a lot, too, while having fun." But parents don't have to make up games. Challenge the kids to make up some. It can bring levity and teach content, too.

Sometimes parents make a really big deal out of certain family dinners. They'll declare a birthday or good report card day or even something silly like Ground Hog Day, as a reason for a special dinner. They'll involve the kids in planning a special menu—light some candles, bring out real cloth napkins. The dinner table is great place to create new traditions. Strive to eat together at least three times a week, but if this is too challenging, possibly start with one night, (maybe Sunday), and work up from there. Everyone attends. Even if they say they are not hungry, they can still talk.

◆ ◆ ◆

Strategy 20:

Family Meetings

Family meetings are a variation of family dinners, but are more formal. They usually have a set agenda and adhere to a set schedule. They typically follow the actual meal.

"We swear by our Family Meetings," said one father. "They bring shape to our frenetic roller-coaster lives. They help keep our fingers on the pulse of what's happening—prevent stuff from falling through the cracks. If I find I'm getting out of touch, I know I can always catch up at the next family meeting. Structured meetings work at the office, so why not at home?"

Some call "family meetings" by other names—family councils, family assemblies, family commissions, family congresses, but the idea and purpose are the same: to keep everyone on the same page and things running smoothly. Some families use a blackboard or whiteboard to track important items. They can be held weekly or monthly—whatever serves the family's needs. One parent described their particular mode:

"Once a week after dinner, we gather for the family meeting. Everyone must attend. No excuses. My wife and I sit at the head of the table, but everyone has a role. We all get to speak, and everyone has a chance to chair a meeting on a rotating basis."

Another shared a slightly different format. "We usually meet once a month. After eating, we clear the table. Then the meeting begins. We acknowledge each other and make eye contact. We review old and new business. Kids can air their issues and ask for help. Everyone gets jobs and we comment on our own observations. We plan events. We note work well done—both in and out of the home. Everyone has a voice. I like knowing that we're giving them a taste of a democracy."

Some of the things discussed at family meetings are:

- Commendations and celebrations. These can range from a pat on the back to a plan to celebrate a major prize or award. Some take turns telling the others what they appreciate about them. One family created their own family victory dance.
- Chores (dissemination and updates)
- Major school projects and when they are due
- Other important assignments or deadlines

- The calendar—immediate upcoming events and long range planning
- Issues among siblings or friends
- Group problem solving (some post a model)
- Other (anyone can ask for an item to be added to the agenda)

"Anyone can add new things. A few months ago, my youngest said he heard about some kids in a nearby county adopting a road, and wondered if we could, too. We brainstormed ideas, then he concluded it was an idea better brought up to his scout troop. The scouts went for it, but our family pitched in to help with the work—cleaning up trash, planting flowers, etc. This month we talked about what seeds we wanted to plant in the garden this spring, and last month we discussed ways to bring down our the electric bill. Even the little ones have opinions. We argue. We debate. But it's always productive."

So much seems to be compromising parental influence these days. The food industry has hijacked our kitchens—largely dictating how and what we eat. The technology industry has hijacked our entire homes—invading every nook and cranny with its virtual presence. It's time to take back some semblance of control. Family meetings are one way to re-seize those reins.

◆ ◆ ◆

Strategy 21:

Goal Setting

An average person with average talent and ambition and average education can outstrip the most brilliant genius in our society, if that person has clear, focused goals.

These words come from the cosmetic maven, Mary Kay, and were passed on at a parenting meeting by a parent who sold her products. The parent wondered why more parents don't seem to make time to sit down with their child and talk about goals and where the future could lead. She believed the cost of not doing so could be great. She wasn't the only one who felt that way, and I joined the group after I came upon a distressing scene in our high school career center.

I was working in a cubicle, adjacent to the High School Career Center, when I became aware of rising voices. A mom, a dad, and a student were "next door" locking horns over what courses the student would take next year.

"Forget it Dad. Just forget it. You're not hearing me. I will not—do you hear me, WILL NOT take Biology II next year." Crouched over some course selection forms, their voices continued to escalate. Both were in a frenzied state, oblivious to others around them, including the mother who was trying to hush them.

"You need this course," the father insisted, pounding on the table. "It will positively give you a leg-up in pre-med. Most top colleges will be looking for this on your transcript."

"I don't care. I'm not taking that course, do you hear? And I'm not going pre-med. Do you hear that, too?" The voice was beyond resolve now—angry and challenging. "N.O."

"How do you expect to become a doctor if you don't stay competitive from the outset? We're trying to help." The mother butted out, and I thought maybe she was crying. I thought about intervening if this didn't come to a halt.

"And who expects to become a doctor? Not me. Have you checked in with me lately? Who says I'm even going to college?"

The mother gasped audibly, as the father seethed through gritted teeth.

"This is most disturbing, Dennis. You know your mother and I have had that dream for years."

"Well, too bad.. You never consulted me. And I have no intention of becoming a doctor. I'm headed for music... the bright lights of New York City. Sorry Mom. I hate to inform you. You won't be able to brag, 'My son, The doctor.' It's just not happening."

The squabble went on for a few more minutes, dissolving into profanities, threats and more tears, and then they suddenly stormed out, papers still in hand.

I knew students sometimes had different goals than their parents, but wasn't prepared for this. It was a sad scene to witness. I knew the student to be a "top dog", probably capable of any course or any career path of his choice: medicine, music, anything he wanted; however, this family hadn't taken time to discuss the future. Each had different goals. Each assumed too much.

Career awareness needs to start early—as early as kindergarten—and possibly even before kindergarten. Parents should talk frequently about the different kinds of jobs people have. They should begin to glean the child's interests and proclivities. They should talk together and dream together—leaving the door open for multiple possibilities, if initial dreams don't materialize, or new horizons appear. Experts agree. Three key points to discuss are:

- What the child likes
- What the child is good at
- Possible matches to what the world needs.

To build common ground over time and avoid surprises such as the one I came upon in the Career Center, it is recommended that parents:

- Study and support children's strengths and needs from the earliest days.

- Feed their interests with books, toys, experiences and special lessons.

- Listen to the children. Engage in numerous two way-conversations about what the child likes, is good at, and what the world may need (employability). Let them know that some jobs of the future haven't even been invented yet. Still, roles cluster around certain competencies, so at least some general focus is a good idea.

- Offer support, encouragement and enthusiasm when they show a special focus.

- Dream together and envision the future in detail. Discuss the pros and cons of different choices.

- Set big long term goals, and lots of small ones which together you can gauge or measure as you go along. Discuss how to move to each subsequent level.

- Celebrate goal attainment at each level.

- Acknowledge that students have the right to change their minds. New options could come along at any juncture. It's familiarization with the overall process that's important.

- Keep a log or journal for each child. Involve the student in this project as early as Middle School. Bring it out and review it from time to time.

Don't be afraid to talk about your own trajectory, including triumphs and bloopers. Kids love to hear about their parents' own track. Just don't be prolonged or repetitive. Let them know that they are your greatest triumphs, and what you ultimately want is their happiness. Some parents also recommend that you:

- Start a clipping file, scrapbook, or memorabilia box related to their strengths—prizes, report card grades, complementary remarks shared by others, etc.

- Access contests and competitions that interest the child and fit along the way.

- Talk about allied careers in case a long range goal doesn't seem to be feasible.

- Develop and share an awareness of career ladders. For example, if a student is interested in a potential medical career, volunteering at a nursing home or hospital will be useful. A potential teacher may want to baby-sit, or tutor at an elementary school or serve as a camp counselor or recreation center to see if working with young people is what he really likes.

- Stay abreast of developing opportunities in the work force. There are always alternatives for those not necessarily bound for a four years college. Some "hot" careers today that don't necessarily require four years of preparation are transportation, hospitality and food service, allied medicine, and nanotechnology, These change frequently, so check with your local community college for reliable and usually free advice.

There is a large body of research that indicates that people who set goals go further in life. Mary Kay is correct. And kids who can't conjure up an image of their future by their teens are often in trouble. Too many will aimlessly drift in and out of courses and careers with a poor overall prognosis. As mentioned, one long term follow-up study of highly gifted students showed that even among that group, those who identified specific interests and set goals early on, had greater career success and life satisfaction than those who hadn't.

Goals are huge—all goals. One study from the University of Tennessee revealed the adverse effects of murky goals. They compared the effects of conflict on Bosnians with vague goals in their 1990's war to the effects on Egyptians with clear goals who fought for democracy in the Arab Spring uprising of 2011. While the losses of both cultures were similar, and the Egyptians possibly were more severe, The Bosnians were far more traumatized by their conflict than the Egyptians. This was so, it is believed, because the Egyptians were clear in why they were fighting, while the Bosnians were not. Clear goals help in many ways.

Don't put off visioning the future and goal setting. Don't wait for that call from the high school guidance counselor to sign up for post secondary planning, nor the eighth grade counselor to broach the Myers-Briggs type-report on interests and proclivities, that is common at that level. Even then it may be too late. Ongoing dialogue about goals will help keep your child motivated and on track.

♦   ♦   ♦

Strategy 22:

Managing Stress

We'll never eliminate stress altogether, nor would we want to. The best we can do is manage it.

Despite all the good habits we may have, we'll never fully escape stress. And that's okay. Stress is healthy and normal. It releases the neurotransmitter norepinephrine, which helps us with decision making—makes us more alert, and sometimes forces us into action. (Think fight or flight. How would our ancestors have escaped those bears and mountain lions without feeling stress?) Stress can also help us create powerful new memories, improve our mood and raise our levels of creative thinking.

But too much stress and norepinephrine can be bad. A chronic dose of it can overload the brain, suppress the immune system, make us sick, and if excessive and prolonged, even kill brain cells.

> Be sure to monitor your own stress, and model and teach some stress busters to your kids. Try some of the following:

- Deep breathing. (Count to five and breathe in. Count to six and breathe out.)
- Visualization. (Picture yourself in a peaceful setting.) Breathe deeply.
- Count backwards slowly from ten.
- Self Talk: "What is the worst thing that could happen if I make this choice—or that choice? Is this really worth worrying about, etc.?
- Reframing a situation: Remind yourself, "No one is perfect. We all slip up. We are all human. Don't worry about the things you can't change. Learn from the *Tao*: It's not what happens outside of you that counts. It's only your reaction that matters."
- Reminding your child that our mistakes are what make us strong
- Listening to calming music
- Creating a piece of art or craft
- Movement: exercise, walking, sweeping the floors, dancing, etc.
- Using stress balls for the hands
- Sleeping
- Prayer
- Meditation

- Yoga, Tai Chi, or Qi Gong
- Treating yourself to a favorite snack, a trinket, or a piece of jewelry, etc.
- Social interaction—especially, finding people who make you laugh
- Creative writing
- Journal writing
- Blogging
- Doodling
- Phoning a friend
- Taking a whiff of lavender or vanilla
- Sipping black tea
- Asserting yourself. Not holding back. Speaking your mind. Being honest.

If you see your teens or pre-teens slipping into bad habits as a result of stress—drugs, alcohol, promiscuous sex, etc., speak openly to them about this. Explain the false lure of using those as a substitute for relieving stress, and note that they will only exacerbate their problems. Keep lines of communication open at all times, encourage wholesome activities, and share some stress busters as noted above.

Give ample freedom to your kids—especially teenagers. Encourage effort and hard work, but don't put too much pressure on them. Overlook some minor infractions. Be aware that teens need a good measure of independence, and long to be incorporated into the real world. Some precocious pre-teens are ready for experiences before their peers. Some experts believe that teens who act out, do so partly because they are resentful that they are not yet been accepted as full members of society. They feel held back in their participation. For example, societies with low or no legal drinking age have more responsible drinkers. In some

European cultures it is more common to treat adolescents as adults, and they are somewhat more easily integrated into those societies. In this country we are just beginning to recognize this. Early admission to college (skipping grades 11 and 12) for mature students who are underachieving sometimes works well. "Middle Colleges," and accelerated tracks to trade schools and community colleges have also become more popular. Online acceleration and cyber-schools work for others, particularly when combined with part-time work.

◆ ◆ ◆

Strategy 23:

Self-Discipline and Parental Discipline

Self Discipline may be the most important gift you can give your child. In the end, we're responsible for ourselves.

Self Discipline:

Years ago researchers used marshmallows to test the self control of four year olds. (They found that children who were able to resist the candy placed in front of them at age four, turned out years later to have higher SAT scores than those who couldn't wait to devour the marshmallow.) The patient children didn't necessarily have a natural gift for patience, but somehow they had learned techniques to control their attention. Some believe that impulsivity is an inherited trait, but parents can help foster self discipline in any child.

> The ability to regulate and control oneself is linked to the ability to focus, concentrate and pay attention, all of which we are learning play a great role in academic success and goal achievement.

Some strategies that slow kids down and encourage the development of self-discipline are:

- board games
- guessing games, such as "I Spy" and "Ghost," and "Twenty Questions"
- games with rules, such as "Red Light, Green Light," or "Simon Says"
- games with changing rules, such as "Simon Says Do the Opposite"
- videogames that require switching of attention (and no violence)
- age-appropriate puzzles
- developing plans and then carrying them out
- making up stories
- playing make-believe in younger children, and creative expression in children of all ages
- engagement in multi-step projects in older children, such as creating an art piece or building something that they enjoy.

Ongoing guidance to children as they work and play helps, too. If they seem a little out of control at times, you may say, "Stop and think before you act," Or, "Try not to blurt things out, because your words could hurt someone's feelings." When they appear bored and want to quit, say something like, "Sometimes we need to keep working through with a project, even though something else seems like more fun. Just stick with the work, and you can have fun later."

Perhaps during a board game, a young child lacking in self-control may be moving his pieces at random. You can say, "You can't move your pieces until it's your turn." These are simple things—and obviously not magic bullets, but they are the kinds of day-to-day things that effective parents can do to help teach their children develop self-discipline.

Again, it helps to observe the child. You can learn how to support him in his frustration. In the infant, for example, experiment to discover what helps him focus or calm himself down when he is upset. Is it holding him tight, or distracting him , or rocking him or singing a soothing song? Once you know this, you can provide the scaffolding that supports the learning process until he is strong enough to stand on his own.

According to psychologists Sam Wang and Sandra Ammodt, "In young children, warm supportive mothering is associated with improved self-control ability, even when the mother's genetic contribution is factored out."

With older children we also want to continue to study their deepest interests and passions. Help feed those passions. The positive feedback they'll get from the joy and success they experience by doing what they most love will encourage greater self-discipline moving forward. Is his first love tae kwon do? Model making? Soccer? Graphic Arts? Whatever it is, support and encourage him in this. You'll see him grow in energy and persistence.

Children who don't do this—those who fail to develop an age-appropriate level of self-discipline and ability to concentrate are likely to get poor grades and be labeled as disruptive, setting up a chain of failure.

Parental Discipline:

But then, again, they are still kids. And sometimes "kids will be kids." They will not always display perfect self-discipline, and sometimes parents need to step in. Oceans of ink have been spent on this topic of discipline, and I suppose oceans more will follow.

The smartest kid I ever knew came up with one of most devious plots imaginable. He conspired with his friends to turn one of their parents' garages into an ice hockey rink by coating the floor with gallons and gallons of olive oil, while they were away for the weekend. "Call as soon as your parents pull away on Friday," he said to one of his "easily led" pals. "I already have my trunk loaded up with gallons of the stuff—there must be forty of them, and as soon as I get the 'all clear' signal, I'll race over and we'll be slippin' and slidin' before you know. Whoo Hoo! Man, it'll be the hockey game of the century!" "Bring it on Dude," the pal whooped, giving the "evil genius" a high five.

"Over my dead body," came a shriek for the next room. Unbeknownst to the conspirators, the parent whose garage was to be "overhauled" was listening from the next room as she wiped down baseboards on her knees. "Scratch that plan," she bellowed, popping up and killing the outrageous plan. She notified the other parents, who each meted out justice, but the story is still told today. I for one, am still in a state of shock—and that was many years ago.

So count on it. Every kid will sow some naughty seeds now and then—or at least try to. And every parent needs to react. The question is this: "How can you best discipline your children without breaking their spirit? Or better yet, how do you raise your children, so you never have to discipline them in the first place? The answer is complex, but for one, it helps to leverage one's natural _authority_ from the beginning. Psychologist Wendy Mogul tells us:

Kids need to learn very early on, who is boss—YOU! So exude your authority—subtly and lovingly—but clearly and definitively. There should be no doubt that the parents are in charge, and in establishing this, your job will be easier going forth.

It's always best to explain exactly what you want the child to do before the child acts—not after he acts. But when things go awry and differences arise, first talk to the child. "What are you doing? (or what did you do?) Why are you doing it?" "Is that the right thing to do? What do you plan to do about it?" Listen to their explanations. If too much damage has not been done, offer them choices for rectifying the situation. If choices are not feasible (and sometimes things are not up for discussion) then you must pull rank and impose consequences. Don't feel guilty. Explain that they are the child and you are the parent, and not meant to be their friend. Sometimes they simply must obey. Deep down inside, everyone—young and old—wants boundaries and reasonable demands to be placed on them.

If you've made the boundaries clear and offered options, and the child still disobeys, parents should impose consequences that are firm, fair, and consistent. (We'll get to that.)

But ideally, fear is downplayed and threats are minimal. To head off trouble in the first place, try to:

- Catch them doing good things.
- Praise them for their efforts. "I love the way you're picking up the toys. It really pleases me when you do your chores without my having to nag. "I'm so proud of the decisions you make. You certainly seem to have your head screwed on right."
- Brag to others a little about their successes—especially grandparents and close friends whom they respect. "She

weeded the whole garden beautifully all summer. I'm so proud of her."

- Ignore some of their smaller infractions, especially if the cost of not doing so, is too high. (Do your own cost benefit analysis of this.)

- Be proactive. Learn their triggers. Prevent clashes. If you know your young child has trouble with transitions and deadlines, for example, give her a heads-up: "We're leaving in ten minutes. Please start to clean up in five." Then give the five minute warning, with a reminder: "Wind the game down now, please, Emma."

Anytime you can encourage and reward positive behavior, you're more apt to be on the same page as your child. Seek balance—a balance of freedom and structure. Once your authority is clear, you can establish a few basic rules and expectations, along with consequences, if they stray. The mutual understanding of these rules and consequences adds to the structure. Then, within the structure, allow freedom. Signal joy and permission to explore. With the right balance of freedom and structure, they should thrive. But it takes some experimentation. It's not always easy to balance freedom with structure—in fact, it's one of the greatest challenges of parenting. Just go on. Exercise your double Dutch, tango and juggling skills. You'll be amazed at the results.

Behavior Plans:

But if the balance of freedom and structure doesn't work out for you and your child, and misbehavior becomes chronic or severe—and sometimes it does—you may want to set up what is now commonly called a "behavior plan." This is a state-of-the art intervention for dealing with sticky little issues or even deeply entrenched aberrant behaviors.

These plans can be simple or complex. At its simplest, it means talking about desired outcomes, and then placing a star or sticker or happy face on a calendar on the days when there are no infractions, and rewarding the improved behavior. Or it can be more complex in serious cases-- requiring deep analysis of causes along with triggers of poor behavior. This is followed by clear goal setting, monitoring and recording of actual behaviors at frequent intervals—and then appropriate responses and consequences. You'll ask: What needs to change? What's most likely to precede the existing misbehavior? And how will you intervene to address that? What data will be gathered, and how will we reward a good outcome? Sometimes parents can develop a plan together. Sometimes schools can gather a team to help develop a plan, or a paid professional is brought in on a case. Behavior plans are excellent ways to shape behavior and usually worth the time and attention to implement them. Again, they can be as simple or complex as desired, involving some or all of the following:

- Clearly define the behaviors that need to change
- Determine triggers that are most likely to precede the existing misbehavior?
- How will they be modified or addressed?
- Set a goal. Be positive. Let the child know you what you want to happen. Explain that you want to work with him on this plan because you care for him and expect him to succeed.
- Discuss some reasonable rewards—these can be anything from a treat, a small toy, to more time on the computer, TV or playing videogames, playdates, incremental boosts in allowances, or even pizzas. Food works well with teens.
- Discuss consequences. Consequences can be loss of existing privileges or failure to attain the anticipated rewards.
- Chart the progress ongoing. Use stickers or stars or check marks (depending on the age) to mark progress at pre-determined intervals.

- Adjust length of intervals to the child.
- Review expectations as you go along. If they falter ask: Was that a good choice or a bad choice? Why? What can you do to improve the next time?
- If the child fails to meet expectations, impose consequences (withdrawal of privileges, etc.).
- Discuss the failure of the plan, and what to do next. One option is to start over with lowered expectations. Ask the child how he would readjust the goal and/or allow him to impose his own outcomes.
- If neither of those works, you can pull back and let natural consequences take over—(the sting of going to school with no homework, for example, may be worse than anything the parent could have done, anyway. Or blowing one's wad of allowance at the mall or on a videogame and not having lunch money for the week, will hurt.)
- Celebrate when goals are met.

The length and/or complexity of behavior management will depend on the age of the child and the circumstances. But they generally work for two reasons: one, they are based on positive inducements; and two, they involve clear observable, measureable data, so all can see when progress is made. Behavior plans have been proven to work in a range of settings—from preschools to prisons. (In correctional facilities, inmates earn cigarettes, extra time in the yard, etc. based on data.) In some cases, the plans may be combined with pharmaceuticals, further increasing their effectiveness. Behavior management plans are today's gold standard in behavior shaping.

Firm, Fair and Consistent:

But again, prevention is always preferable. One "oldie, but goodie" philosophy for disciplining children is the "Firm, Fair.

and Consistent" model—a good guide for all ages and stages of development.

Firm: Clarify expectations, then if there are serious transgressions, and you've used some of the strategies above, pull rank. Immediately. No mixed messages. An eight month old needs to hear and understand "NO," when he's cruising toward a dangerous object. A five years old needs to understand "NO," when he begins to dart into traffic. Pre-teens need to be reined in when begin to spout bad language or backtalk, and teenagers who abuse curfews and driving privileges, need to know they may lose those privileges. "No," and a quick reminder of the ground-rules often works well.

Fair: Kids have the right to know rationales of what is expected of them. Again, clear boundaries need to be set, and discussed with the child *before* they start of think of infractions. Talk about reasons why we need rules—for safety and order. Be realistic. Don't ask the child to do what he can't do. When infractions occur, the punishment needs to fit the crime. Time-outs are often effective with young children. The rule of thumb is one minute in time-out for each year of age. (A four year old should be expected to sit in time-out for four minutes.) Withdrawal of privileges is a common way to punish older children. No car this weekend. A stricter curfew. No sleepovers or trips to the mall.

Consistent: Reward conformity and punish infractions. Follow through religiously. Review rules at family dinners and meetings. (Make sure you and your partner are on the same page.) Know what motivates your child: hugs, high fives, special activities, computer time, pizza, etc, and use these spontaneously and liberally when you feel proud. Repeat offenders may need extra help. Involve your child in developing a behavior plan, such as discussed.

Firm, Fair, and Consistent are excellent words for any parent to commit to memory, but like other suggestions from parents and experts, they may require reflection and some adjustments on the part of parents

"I Messages" is yet another "oldie but goodie" model worthy of note. I like it because again, the emphasis is on "prevention" of misbehavior. The model stems from the work of Dr. Haim Ginnot and is fairly easy to learn. "I Messages" work because they share feelings without blame, and keep the emphasis on the positive.

Here's the formula. The parent says the following:

"I feel" _____ ("upset" or "sad" or "disappointed," etc.—whatever fits). (Fill in the blank with your own feeling.)

"When" _____ (Give a reason—e.g, "you play your music so loud," or "you leave your toys strewn all over the floor," etc. or whatever is frustrating you.) Then follow with:

"Because" _____ (Explain the effects of the misbehavior—such as "I can't concentrate on my work, so I'd like you to turn it down," or "Someone could trip on your toys and get hurt," etc.)

Commit it to memory if you can:

I feel... when... because... This is all you have to remember. Fill in the blanks with the situation. When parents use "I messages," they teach children that other people have feelings, too, and they model an effective way for children to deal with their own feelings, as behavior improves, and escalations are prevented.

Chapter 6:
The Cognitive Domain

INTRODUCTION:

To some, the cognitive realm represents the "meat" of the matter. It refers to the academics—the intellectual realm. It's the reason some picked this book up in the first place. And for those folks, "beefing up" the cognitive is the key to a child's success. But a word to the wise: While the cognitive realm is important, it never truly stands alone. It cannot. No student will ever fully develop if the focus is purely intellectual, because all domains are meant to be connected, integrated, and supported by the others.

That said, it's still natural to be curious about intelligence and academics. Who hasn't wondered, what is intelligence? What makes some kids smarter than others? How can parents and others best tap that source? This is where we began, and where we now pick up.

Remember, a new view of intelligence has emerged. Intelligence is not a fixed trait, but a process. We can become smarter tomorrow than we are today. Each of us moves along a continuum as we are challenged. Anyone can become more intelligent and more talented in various ways.

One may say we are all works in progress. None of us is born with a brain that is completed. By nature we are changeable, malleable, plastic, and we can be rewired. A certain degree of cognitive growth happens naturally through maturation and the instinctive actions of our caregivers. But additionally, through our own force of will we can add to that. If we are intentional, we can flip internal switches and turn unseen knobs in ourselves and in our children that can fire up neurons and alter genes beyond the normal scope. Every day and in every way we have opportunities to allow our environment to change us and our children. Experiences add up. And positive and enriching ones extend our intellectual capacity. No one knows what limits we possess.

- According to psychologist, Robert Sternberg, one of the world's leading psychologists, "One moves along the continuum as one acquires a broader range of skills, or reaches a deeper level of the skills one already has, or increases in the efficiency in the utilization of existing skills."

- Psychiatrist Leon Eisenberg and collaborators say that "The cortex (the brain's seat of higher learning) has a remarkable capacity for remodeling according to environmental change."

- Harvard's Howard Gardner describes intelligence as a "bio-psychological potential, and has identified at least nine different kinds of intelligence." Some suspect there are many more.

- Researchers Ceci, Rostenblum, deBruyn, and Lee say: "We have no way of knowing how much unactualized genetic potential exists."

One recent study showed that IQ in teens could be raised by as much as 20 points in as little as four years. The dial in those teens, therefore, moved from the "average" to "gifted" range. Some believe that even greater increases are possible—as many as forty IQ points. But no one knows for sure. Development of talent—academic or otherwise—is now viewed as the result of slow, sustained, and intense effort over time. According to Shenk, every human brain has a built-in capacity to become over time what we demand of it.

I've personally seen students who did not test as "gifted" in the early grades, ascend to the top of the class and graduate as valedictorians or salutatorians. I've also happily witnessed learning disabled students overcome disabilities, excel in specific areas, and go on to be accepted to selective colleges.

But IQ tests are not without their limitations. Through the years, they have been faulted for their many shortcomings, such as cultural bias, etc.—some of which still exist; but now those are more widely acknowledged. And thankfully, the tests are used less for sorting and labeling, but more appropriately for diagnostic and remedial purposes. Some would like to see intelligence testing end altogether, but that is unlikely to happen, for strong market forces, the need for diagnostic tools, and other reasons preclude that.

This hasn't stopped some entrepreneurs from spotting an opportunity, though. With the acknowledgement of human plasticity and its potential, some are determined to make everyone smarter. They've come out with many products and gimmicks aimed at boosting IQ. Pills, supplements, brain training programs, software, gadgets and various practices have been offered to the public as means to sharpen brains. The question is: Do they work? And if so, how does one know which are better than others? How does one separate the good from the bad? The public has often been confused, so the National Institutes of Health (NIH) stepped in to help evaluate some claims. In 2010 they assessed the effectiveness of many of the major theories to see what works.

The jury is still out in many cases; however, three stood up to the most rigorous standards. They were:

- Physical exercise
- Meditation
- Some videogames

Physical exercise was probably the least surprising; meditation was of some surprise to a few; and non-violent videogames, often given a "bad rap", were exonerated to an extent.

Only two videogames, though, actually passed the rigorous tests, and these were specifically geared for older adults—namely, "Space Fortress," and "Rise of Nations." While neither game is seen as appropriate for young children (the study was mostly aimed at preventing cognitive decline in adults), there is, nonetheless, some evidence that games that require switching, and ascending demands on attention and focus "probably do the most good," and this may include games for children. Subsequent tests hinted that this is true.

What were not tested, however, were many of the tried and true cognitive favorites—some long standing practices that parents have used for centuries to mold youngsters' minds. Strategies such as critical and creative thinking skills, questioning and problem solving models, memory training, etc. have endured through the ages, and though not studied recently by the NIH, parents have weighed in on them, and confirmed their effectiveness. These strategies are what we will discuss later in this chapter.

Sometimes schools use the strategies described, too. But more often than not, most are not emphasized directly. Schools are very busy with mandated curricula. They don't always have the time to teach a breadth of thinking skills that is desirable. But the real world demands these competencies. In fact, certain skills, such as problem solving and critical thinking are more related to day-to-day success than skills taught in many academic courses. It's good for parents to be aware of this, so they can supplement and complement what the schools are doing as they go along.

Without systematic input and training, some neuroscientists say that brains will grow in haphazard ways. This is not ideal. Brain training, which parents can foster, is preferable. Brain training can help prevent that haphazard pattern.

> Interventions, such as setting a positive climate, pouring on rich language, and knowing how to work with one's schools, can further help make the most of learning. Sometimes it's the little things that matter.

Other times, some effort and thought on the part of the parent is needed. If you add in a "can do" mindset, and an eye for PACT balance, the advantage will be in your child's court.

A HAP once made this point: Everything in the physical universe tends toward disorder. If we don't clean our houses, they get messy. If we don't weed our gardens, they become overgrown. If we don't stimulate and train our minds they, too, become weak or grow haphazardly. This is another reason to actively work with our children and keep them sharp.

◆ ◆ ◆

Strategy 24:

Climate

We, as parents are in charge of the home's climate. We set the tone. We control the circumstances of learning. But sometimes we forget that.

Not much learning occurs if we are forced to learn. Who wants content jammed down their throats? No one. Not even laboratory animals. As Dr. Fred Gage's studies at the Salk Institute in California showed: rats who were voluntarily permitted to run and exercise on wheels exceeded expectations, while comparable rats that were forced to exercise, fared far more poorly. Humans show the same tendencies. We generally learn better on our own terms.

Joy, awe, and wonderment and freedom can draw that learning out. Don't you prefer to be lured into an exciting-looking activity, than forcefully mandated to partake? Well, kids are the same. That's how kids learn best, too.

Not that all children are natural willing learners in all areas and at all times. Sometimes you must entice them to move toward the bait. But that's okay. Go on. Coax them a little.

"What? No way. You don't get my kids," one father objected when that idea was thrown out. "They have to be practically beaten down the road with a stick to do any work. My kids will sit on their butts or drag their feet every chance they get. They don't want to learn. They can be oppositional, contrary, grumpy, slow moving, bleary eyed, lethargic, and disinterested—moaning and groaning when asked to do the simplest things. Yesterday, when I tried to compare the monetary advantages of one part-time job over the other, my son just looked at me blankly and said 'What the hell are you talking about, Dude? I know what's best for me. I can count to ten.'… And you're saying I'm supposed to sugar coat things for him.? Show glee? Exude joy? Are you crazy? You don't know teenagers."

Well, it's true—sometimes teens react like that. It's their temporary disability. It's called adolescence. But this, too, shall pass. Sometimes you just have to walk away from them for awhile. Ignore them. Come back later. But meanwhile, be joyful despite them. That's our job. We're the adults. They're the ones under siege by their hormones. So just ignore the eye rolling, overlook the contempt and bounce back from their moods. Maintain your own happy mood. That's what being a parent means sometimes. If your children are still young, prepare for it.

"Whatever happened to those jubilant babies who reveled in our every word, followed all our movements and laughed at our silly faces?" a mother of a teen asked. Well, it hasn't gone totally. It's still there. In adolescence, it sometimes temporarily goes underground. But it will return. Just stay the course. For those same delightful people really do still live in your home. They just wax and wane at times—disappear from view, then reappear again with vigor and shared excitement—sometimes when we least expect it. Have patience. Pay them no mind. Just go on talking about exciting things, thrilling ideas, and spreading your own joy around. They'll pretend that they're not listening or they don't care, but amazingly a lot of it will seep in and stick.

> Above all, resolve to be alive. Vow to be happy and cheerful yourself—even when they are not. Know that the interjection of your ideas and happy experiences can energize them beneath those bad moods.

- Express your excitement about a story line of a book, movie, or TV show you've seen.
- Plan an outing.
- Discuss interesting upbeat current events.
- Share insights you have about community events.

Some topics will be contagious and overall, you will be building a positive and intellectual climate in the home. Families with successful students delight in the sharing of ideas—even when the kids appear temporarily tuned out. Eventually your own awe, curiosity and enthusiasm will shine through, and take root.

It's up to the parents to take charge of your home's tone. Set the course. Turn the ship around if it's going in a direction that does not please you. But above all:

- Choose joy. Wake up happy. Talk. Play.
- Seek out the wonder. Find the bliss. Respond to the day with joy and gratitude.
- Clap and dance and sing and drum. Laugh out loud every chance you get.
- Refuse to acknowledge the grumbles in your midst.
- Ignore the eye-rolling and heavy sighs. For these, too shall pass. (Employ the old expression: "Just moving right along.")
- If effusion is not your thing, share respect and simple awe.
- Whatever your style, just let your strong emotions hang out there.

One mother backed me up on this topic: "I personally recommend to other mothers, that we let it all hang out there. It's our job to hug and kiss the kids, and let them know what a big wide wonderful world they live in—filled with majesty and awesomeness—and how happy you are to share it with them. I never hold back. When they accuse me of being weird or embarrassing, I just overlook it. When they say something's not cool, I feign deafness. I always make a point to respond with kindness and patience. They eventually come around. And I notice that little by little they are turning out to be happy and affectionate people in their own right."

Of course, moods run the full gamut, and vary with the individual, but they all leave an impression. Sometimes it's the memories that impact the child's upbringing.

One man spoke of his father's deep response to literature and the effects it had on him:

"Every Christmas Eve, my father read passages from Dickens' *Christmas Carol*. His tone, his demeanor, his reverence moved me to the core. I was deeply impacted. I sensed this was something very beautiful and important, and the impression stayed with me through the years. In turn, the power of literature is something I want to pass on. I think that's part of the reason I became an English teacher and enjoy it so much."

Always go for the drama. Climate plays a great role in learning and retention, as well as becoming who we are.

◆ ◆ ◆

Strategy 25:

Making Connections

Being able to make connections underscores "aha" moments in math, science, social studies, language—and virtually every system one can think of. But it takes practice. Giving children practice making connections prepares them for higher order thinking.

Anyone who ever watched Sesame Street is bound to remember this jingle: "One of these things is not like the other, one of these letters just isn't the same... " I confess I found it irksome at the time. Over and over the pesky jingle rang out from the television set—much to my toddler's delight and to my annoyance. I would turn the set off if such an action had not caused an uproar. And that was just the beginning. My daughter then went around grouping objects and singing aloud as her toys and props "connected." What I didn't know was that from that simple jingle and game, a long upward slope of similar games and connecting abilities was taking root.

It wasn't until high school that I discovered there was a payoff: One day she came home and announced that the history teacher had given a pop quiz. "We had to compare Han China with the Holy Roman Empire, and then contrast Francis Bacon's Authority of Experience to Descartes Authority of Reason." "Whoa," I commented, a little taken back. "A piece of cake, Mom," she reassured. "I aced it... I'm really good at this compare and contrast stuff. I can make connections between almost anything." Thank you, Elmo and Joan Ganz Cooney!

Harvard's Elizabeth Spelke's performed a study that shows that babies' ability to categorize emerges at a much earlier age than was previously thought. Much of the ability to categorize is built into the baby's brain, but parents can help develop and accelerate this natural proclivity, which can lead to valuable academic skills.

Direct baby's attention to patterns and connections:

- Have baby match his toy with a toy from a different group.
- Ask toddlers to match socks, toys, barrettes, coins, pictures.
- Find similar animals or figures on their clothing on sheets.
- String beads and macaroni, matching mom or dad's pattern: "Blue. Yellow. White. Blue. Yellow. White."
- Ask: "How are these animals alike? Different?"
- Circle all the shapes that go together. Pat an X on the one that doesn't belong.

(Kid's menus, magazines, workbooks and Dollar Store coloring books are filled with activities with variations on pattern finding. Don't discount their value.) As the child grows, continue to probe for similarities but expand to those that are not necessarily clear:

- Let's lay back and watch these clouds go by. What do they look like?
- How are these pliers like a lobster? How is a hummingbird like a helicopter?
- Have kids finish the pattern of a tune—Or a pattern in a piece of artwork
- Compare favorite styles of vocalists and actors.
- Seek similarities in themes of films or TV shows or videogames
- Ask: How are the characters in this book alike and different? Do we know anyone like that?
- How can we connect *Star Wars* with *Avatar*? *Romeo and Juliet* with *West Side Story*?

There are many ways to actively probe for similarities and differences in the world around us every day, and there is not a discipline that won't be enhanced by the ability to quickly spot patterns and make connections. Success in math, science, social studies and language require the ability of one to apply one's skills of making connections. When that connection occurs, "Aha!" How sweet those moments are!

Finding patterns and making connections early on sets the stage for many higher order skills later. The slope typically begins slowly. If feedback is positive, it will progress steadily as each layer of difficulty leads to the next. Before you know it, your child will be generating insightful analogies, creative metaphors and similes, and blowing the lid off his exams.

◆ ◆ ◆

Strategy 26:

Critical Thinking

Children must be taught to think clearly and rationally.
And they need practice. It doesn't necessarily come with the
package. The mind must be trained how to learn to learn.

In high performing families, parents train children to reason well and to be good critical thinkers all the time. Sometimes the training is direct. Sometimes, it's inadvertent or incidental, such as during projects: "Let's see if this will work—or if that will work." Often the reasoning is modeled using many open-ended questions as they go along.

A few years back, I was on a bus when I overheard a mother and daughter arguing about whether or not the girl should have her own cell phone:

"So what makes you think you're old enough to have one?"

"I'm almost eleven. All the kids I know who are eleven have cell phones."

"And who, pray tell, will pay for it?"

"I will. I have some money saved up, and I might get more money for my birthday."

"And when the money runs out?"

"I'll get a job. By then, I'll be old enough to baby sit."

"And what about the monthly fee? Have you thought about that?"

The volley continued. I stayed tuned because I enjoyed the banter, and was taking notes on how the mother was drawing out the girl's reasoning skills. It was a classic example of critical thinking, though I'm sure the mother didn't realize she was training her daughter's brain at the time.

Some parents may have shut the girl down at this point, viewing her as a brat. But this mother appreciated her daughter's negotiating abilities. I gave it high marks.

Like a ping pong match, the action ensued. Point Counterpoint. Point. Counterpoint.

"What if you lose it?" "I won't. When was the last time I lost something—years!" "It might get stolen... Then who will replace it?" "I will." "What about your brother? He's older and he doesn't have a cell phone yet." "But he doesn't care so much about a phone. And I do. And when he does, maybe he can save up his money, too."

The girl had an answer for each query—definitely a future litigator in training. I wished I had a tape recorder. But I didn't need it, because the conversation stayed with me for several years now. I'm not sure who won the debate—maybe the mother. But one thing I knew for sure was that it was an excellent exercise in critical thinking. So from that perspective, the daughter won.

> Parents who involve their children in discussions where they pick an issue apart, encouraging analysis and even dissent—are training their kids to become deep thinkers.

In many families of high achievers this is a very common practice. When an issue of interest comes up, the parent will play the devil's advocate. "So why should I believe you? What makes you so sure? Maybe the opposite is true. Convince me. Prove it." They encourage the children to defend their positions—to spot relevant issues, to reason, to argue and debate and to communicate with precision. By teaching them to delve deeply and slow things down, we usually get to the root of the matter. And when critical thinking is done respectfully, it is accepted—even welcomed—because parents know it is a powerful learning tool.

Knowing how to think critically is a hallmark of an educated person. It helps one become a more effective communicator, citizen, consumer, decision-maker and problem solver. These are qualities of the intellect that we all want for our children.

Perhaps you've seen the play or movie, "Fiddler on the Roof." In the story, the lead character Tyve, a Jewish Milkman, harrows over how to react to his daughters' disregard for tradition. He talks to God—even argues with God at certain points. "On one hand… " (meaning I can see it your way—and he'll make a point). "But on the other hand… " (He'll reconsider: Can you see it my way?) Back and forth he deliberates, looking at the issue from one perspective, then from another—weighing the merits, pulling it apart, trying to come to a fair conclusion. To some, this may seem like a waste of time. To others, it's a rigorous intellectual event—refining thoughts and comprising the essence of critical thinking. Excellent cognitive training!

Much happens in the normal course of conversation—not unlike the mother and daughter on the bus, "arguing" about the girl having a cell phone. Overall, this brand of critical thinking:

- Encourages students to dig deep.
- Lets children know that it is okay to argue and debate if it's done respectfully.
- Draws upon one's own guidelines.
- Trains their minds.

So model critical thinking. Think aloud when you have decisions to make yourself. Argue out loud with yourself at times and let the kids pick up on the rhythm and rhyme.

"On one hand," this may seem odd or overly indulgent to some—particularly those who believe that children are to be seen and not heard. "On the other hand" if you want strong critical thinkers, model these techniques. They're tried and true. So take your pick.

◆　◆　◆

Strategy 27:

Problem Solving

The problem solving model is as old as the hills—but still an indispensable nugget, as far as I'm concerned. I was trained in it at work. Then I brought it home, and now we all use it.

Problem solving is a particular type of critical thinking; it's also a methodology to help strengthen the mind, and sort out complicated matters. The eminent educational philosopher, John Dewey, is generally credited with introducing the model in the last century. Since then it's taken root in schools, in business and industry—in virtually every setting, because people are always looking for a ways to simplify issues and bring order out of chaos. There are numerous versions of the model nowadays, but are all variations of these basic steps:

John Dewey Problem Solving Model:

1. Identify the problem. (Define the dilemma.)

2. Brainstorm some solutions. (List them.)

3. Weigh the pros and cons of each solution. (Pull things apart, then list the pluses and minuses.)

4. Pick your best choice. Implement it, and then evaluate it. (If later you're not pleased with the outcome, start over again.)

As an example, a mom shared her daughter's dilemma, and how they worked through it. She was accepted to her top two college choices—one at an Ivy League university, and one to a prestigious honors program at the state university. But she couldn't make up her mind. Together they applied the steps of the problem solving model and worked through it.

1. Identify the problem. "She's been accepted to several colleges, and has narrowed her choices to two: State College (reasonable and good) or an Ivy (prestigious, but expensive). She doesn't know which to pick."

2. Brainstorm some solutions. "We listed the major considerations to help pick the best solution: academic fit, costs, distance from home, social stressors, distance from boyfriends' college, distance from friends' colleges, social life, extra-curricular offerings, time for leisure, availability of part time work, and positioning for graduate school after graduation."

3. Weigh the pros and cons of each. "We discussed each consideration in detail, then created a chart with pluses or minuses for each one. That gave weight to each and brought them into better focus."

4. Pick one. Implement it. "We reviewed all our data, then made a decision—State U. We listed next steps and implemented them: notified the colleges of her decision ; sent in the deposit; Tracked all key dates. After a semester, she'll evaluate her choice, and proceed accordingly." "I can always transfer later, if I think I've made the wrong choice," the girl reasoned.

Voila! Simple. Effective. Practical. An easy and systematic way to get one's arms around a complex problem!

Occasionally the problem solving model gets taught in school—but more often than not, it does not. Most schools are too overwhelmed by academic requirements to fit it in. But if schools can't, then their parents should consider it.

A recent study by the Gates Foundation, "Measures of Effective Teaching," revealed that teachers got higher scores on procedural tasks like planning and behavior management, but relatively low scores on fostering analysis and problem solving. So teachers, themselves, it seems, could probably use some training in a problem solving model, as well practice passing it on to their students.

One parent devotee had this to say: "The John Dewey Problem Solving Model is simple to learn and easy to commit to memory. Once you do that, it's yours--a little nugget you can retrieve on demand if you're baffled and in need of a simple template to guide you. It's not unlike some other automatic rules you've tucked away—basic spelling rules, grammar rules, the ten commandments, Roberts' Rules, The Golden Rule, the times tables, "Thirty Days has September," etc.—or any other useful mnemonic."

◆ ◆ ◆

Strategy 28:

Questioning Techniques

Posing good questions activates learning. It's too easy to just skim the surface. So I had to learn to ask good questions to stimulate their minds.

"I think that the single most important thing that teachers and parents do to help kids learn to build brain power is to engage them in meaningful conversations based on questions," says Howard Sternberg, one of the nation's leading authorities on human intelligence. He calls questions "golden opportunities to learn and think." As you may have noticed, a line of questions is built into critical thinking exercises as well as the problem solving model. But more often than not, questions just stand on their own. And then, it's helpful to be able to discern good questions from weaker ones. Learning to craft stimulating questions to activate young minds is a very valuable tool for parents to know and use.

Some parents get annoyed by their children's questions. They think they ask too many, or they're just being pesky and looking for attention. But that's seldom the case. Questions are a good thing. We should not shy away from questions, but welcome them. Even God was questioned. God said to Job, "Question me and I will answer you." So he did. David, Abraham and Jonah also had questions for God. And God answered them, too. And each grew in wisdom and knowledge. So how bad can questions be?

Here are a few general rules from today's experts:

- Encourage questions.
- Respond to some questions with more questions.
- Give *wait time* after a question is asked.
- Vary responses.
- Even if you know the answer to a question, sometimes say, "I'm not sure. Let's look it up." Then do.
- Never show annoyance at questions. Praise them. Let kids know that asking questions is a good thing, and one way to help us learn.
- Ask open-ended questions—questions that have no right or wrong answers.

Expect of course, that they'll have lots of questions themselves, especially the "who, what, why, when, where, and how" variety. Answer them patiently. Also, mix up the kinds of questions you ask your children. Try some of the following:

Essential Questions:

"Essential Questions" are those that revolve around "big ideas"—love and hate, war and peace, courage and cowardice, joy and grief. Ask the child, "What is love," etc. "What is its nature?" "Where does it come from?" "What impact does it have on people in general?... Or on you, in particular?" You dignify children when you pose such questions. You may also want to ask:

What does love look like? How many kinds of love can you think of?

What is war and why do people wage it?

Is there more than one kind of war? Explain.

What does peace mean to you? Could there be such a thing such as too much peace?

What is the meaning of courage? Freedom? Tolerance?

A good time to pose essential questions is when you're reading a book, or watching a TV show or movie and you pick up a theme. Hit "pause" on the remote. Then throw out an essential question. Or wait until the end of the DVD, to ask a salient question. You may be amazed at the child's reaction. Essential questions generally provoke deep thought.

Some other essential questions that you could pose to older children are:

What does it mean to be alive? Truly alive?

Can life and death co-exist? How?

Is loyalty always a positive trait?

Can you think of a situation where betrayal may be a good thing?

What is the meaning of education?

What is a good education?

What is a bad education?

Is it possible to get a good education in a very poor country? Why or Why not?

Some kids might look at you like you're a little crazy at first, but they'll get used to it, and then I think you'll find that they like it. For sure it will stimulate a lot of brain cells. How else are you going to get kids to think if you don't practice?

Bloom's Taxonomy

Psychologist Benjamin Bloom defined a hierarchy of questions to train minds and provoke levels of thought. This pyramid, as his model is called, is known as "Bloom's Taxonomy. " It outlines the least rigorous to the most rigorous types of questions, and helps us to distinguish and categorize them.

> Kids need practice responding to a variety of different kinds of questions. They generally get asked a lot of factual questions, but if you want to promote the deepest thinking of all, concentrate on Bloom's last three types. These are what psychologists call: higher order questions.

Higher order questions force a student to think deeply and really get those neurons chattering away and multiplying.

Most teachers have training in Bloom's Taxonomy. It's a mainstay of pedagogical curriculum. (If it's good for teachers, then you know it's probably good for parents, too.) Teachers are urged to use Bloom's Taxonomy as a guide in planning their lessons, and for differentiating to meet different student's needs. Parents who wish to train their child to think more critically, creatively and deeply may want to learn this and use it when they pose questions to their children. The levels from least to most intellectually demanding are:

1. **Knowledge** questions. These involve facts. They're the easiest questions to come up with. For example, one might ask: "What is the name of the tallest dinosaur?" Knowledge questions are necessary at times, but definitely the least taxing on the intellect.

2. **Comprehension** questions. These check for understanding— e.g., "What is the main reason why dinosaurs no longer roam the earth?" A student has to move past recall, and think more deeply to answer.

3. **Application** questions: Students must apply what they know. "Can you build a diorama to show the environment of Tyrannosaurus Rex?" In other words, prove what you know by showing me.

4. **Analysis** questions: These can get even more demanding. Therefore, they're called "higher order" questions—along with

the next two: synthesis and evaluation. (They require more thought on the part of the adult.) In analysis you're asking a student to take their knowledge apart—e.g., "Can you put all these dinosaurs into categories for me?"

5. **Synthesis** questions are even more difficult yet to answer. They require a student to put pieces of knowledge back together again—e.g., "Can you create a new dinosaur for the Cretaceous Period and name it?"

6. **Evaluation** questions. These are the most rigorous of all. Students must make a judgment and justify it, based on available knowledge and some criteria. —e.g., "Does Tyrannosaurus Rex deserve the title: King of the Dinosaurs? Explain." Deep thought is required to evaluate.

Don't settle for questions just at the knowledge level—e.g., "What's the capital of Nebraska?" "On what date did Washington cross the Delaware?" Or "How do you spell "Mississippi?" Dig deeper. Instead of stopping at "Where did you go?" ask "What did you learn?" "Tell me about it." Ask, "what, if anything would you do differently the next time?" etc. Know the different kinds of questions, and how to craft them. Mix them up. To really exercise the brain, ask some of the most rigorous ones—analysis, synthesis, and evaluation-types. Children will have to probe and you'll be exercising your own gray matter, as well, by having to come up with them.

The Socratic Method

The Socratic Method was first implemented by Socrates, teacher to both Plato and Aristotle. The Socratic Method has stood the test of time as a teaching tool. It's a variation on critical thinking, and another great way to help train young minds. Jesuit institutions used it through the middle ages, and still do today. So do many law schools. And certain colleges have developed their whole core curriculum around this methodology. The Great Books Program is also based on this pedagogy.

Anyone can learn the Socratic Method. It's not difficult, and like John Dewey's problem solving model, it helps develop both creative and critical thinking.

In the Socratic Method, a parent or teacher asks lots and lots of questions. The goal is to have the student ultimately answer his own questions. Through reflection a student is drawn deeper and deeper into an issue, and must justify his position, while thinking about consequences and alternatives. In so doing, the brain is being trained. Often the questioner plays the role of devil's advocate, but ultimately it is the student who is held accountable for his own reasoning.

The process can be used with very young children, as well as very sophisticated students. You can almost see the wheels turning in the child's head when you bring him along with a line of questioning. They usually enjoy it. The mind is learning to become more disciplined and accountable; haphazard thinking is disallowed and there's almost no limit to the learning.

The method has set components. An example of a sequence with a young child may look something like this:

1. QUESTION: (For instance): "Tell me, Susie. Who do you think is the prettiest fairytale princess?"

2. SILENCE: The questioner would then give wait time... (Sample): "Hmmmm. Snow White.")

3. A DECLARATIVE STATEMENT: "So. You think Snow White is the prettiest."

4. A REFLECTIVE STATEMENT: (The questioner pauses again and reflects before affirming): "There is certainly something about her coloring that is unusual and beautiful. It's different from some princesses, isn't it?"

5. <u>ELABORATION</u>: "But tell me more. Why do *you* think so? What are some other things about Snow White that make her seem pretty to *you*?"

6. <u>BRAINSTORMING</u>: "I like her clothes. She has pretty hair. She dances nice. I like the color of her eyes. She smiles a lot. She sings beautiful songs. She is kind. She takes good care of the dwarfs."

The questioner may ask more questions, designed to draw out more information, elicit other possibilities and/or justify the judgment. The child is being trained to think more deeply and to reason, and justify her thoughts. She's learning that details are important.

The same process can be used with older students. For example, after watching the play Hamlet with a teenager, a parent may ask: "What kinds of things is *Hamlet* questioning throughout this play?" Again, the same sequence is followed. The questioner would provide silence, a declarative statement, a reflective statement, invite elaboration and brainstorming. Questions are used to probe:

"How do you know that?"

"Can you explain that a little more?"

"Is the point you are making that… ?"

"What is your reason for saying that?"

"Is it possible that… ?"

"Are there other ways of looking at this?"

"How else could we view this matter?"

The student gets a good grilling as the questioner presses for deeper and deeper reasoning, elaboration, and justification for the statements. And again, the student's mind is being trained (without his knowing it) in critical thinking skills. Not everybody gives much thought to this, but a little practice in honing one's questioning skills can go a long way.

◆   ◆   ◆

Strategy 29:

Memory

A good memory is essential for success in all subjects.
The demands start slow, but keep piling up.

There are two primary types of memory: Working memory and long term memory. Working memory is the ability to keep information in mind for a short time (20–30 seconds—such as remembering the phone number you just looked up); and long term memory, which refers to the continual storage of information, largely outside of our awareness, that can be called up when needed. It is mostly long term memory that we're concerned with here.

When one recalls content, new foundations are built, and new knowledge develops.

> The value of a powerful memory has long been considered a component of high intelligence and essential to knowledge acquisition.

People in ancient Greece and other countries used to memorize vast amounts of information because they had no other way to pass on their culture. And through the ages, people were encouraged to memorize long tracts because they believed this would exercise, cultivate and strengthen minds. This is true. Modern neuroscience has proven that they were right. For example, Buddhist monks start as small children to memorize great tracts of material, and recent examination of their brains has revealed that they have some of the most powerful minds examined by neuroscientists. In 2000, an American, Dr. Eric Kandel, was honored with a Nobel Prize for his work explaining the molecular underpinnings of human memory, and its relationship to neuroplasticity. According to Kandel, brain cells change to store memories.

When Anders Ericsson showed in 1980 that he could take a very average student and train his memory to do phenomenal things, the world took notice. The hope rose that if the secret was in the training, then perhaps a strong memory could belong to anyone. Follow-up studies showed this to be true.

But not all are impressed. Some still besmirch memory training. They call it "robotic" or "mechanistic" and "a waste of time." They claim it's more suitable for circus animals than human beings—that it's diminishing to the person. But they couldn't be more wrong. The work of Kandel and others reveal that long-term memory training, in particular can actually expand whole regions of the brain—a phenomenon heretofore regarded as impossible. Sharon Begley calls memory training "Miracle Gro for the Brain."

On a day-to-day level, many factors affect memory:

- Emotionally charged events. These help us remember more facts than dull ones. Positive events, in particular, invoke more details.
- Mood. Studies show this affects what is encoded and retrieved in memory. (Think the "Gaze," and the "Touch." Positive physical impressions and associations may foster the encoding of content.)

- Sleep. Disturbances in sleep hurt memory consolidation. But now we've learned that sound sleep after learning is most effective. Naps after a study help with later recall.

- Nutrition. Food and drink count in how well we remember. A high fructose diet, for example, directly impairs brain function and memory. (Check labels for corn syrup—a particular culprit and included in many foods these days.)

- Multi-tasking. Most think this is a good thing. But scientists who have studied it, say multi-tasking interferes with memory. Multi-tasking should not be encouraged.

- Novel and the Complex events. These help build memory power. In a famous study of London taxicab drivers, it was discovered that the inadvertent training required to traverse highly complicated streets and neighborhoods on the job, expanded their brains. Scientific imaging confirmed this. For those of us not planning to move to London to switch careers, other types of travel can offer an option. We're often forced to cope with new sights and sounds, as well as strange languages and customs. As we strain to do so, we tax our memories and simultaneously build new brain capacity. If we can't travel, experts recommend we spend fifteen minutes a day learning and memorizing something new—a skill, a language, a dance routine, etc.

- Spacing. Spacing out study sessions over time helps fix material firmly in our minds.

Commonly, parents of successful students say they started early to train their children's memory:

"We repeated nursery rhymes over and over. We sang simple songs, and played games such as 'Simon Says,' or 'I'm going to Texas,' where each person adds to a growing list of objects. We had fun. We sang songs like *'Old McDonald,' 'If You're Happy and*

You Know It,' 'I Know An Old Woman who Swallowed a Fly,' 'She'll Be Comin' Round the Mountain,' 'Twelve Days of Christmas,' and others that require one to remember a string of words. My own memory got a good workout, too." (We always suspected this was good for young brains, though we had no firm evidence that this is so; but today we do.)

No one will do well in school without a good memory. Every subject requires it. From the early grades, students must memorize sight words and spelling words, number facts, and important dates from history. A little later they'll be asked to rattle off the capitals of states and countries, math formulas, leading characters in books and plot summaries. There's no let up. It goes on. Memorization of math formulas, plant and animal taxonomies, chemical valences and causes of wars are required. Demands are dizzying and unrelenting.

So start early to get them ready and train their brains in this regard. Some additional ideas for strengthening memory in younger children are:

- Story retelling: Read a book. Watch a movie. Ask your child to retell the plot—then the names of the characters, interesting props or other details.

- Memorizing poetry or short passages of literature. (Seasonal ones work well.) Recite for the family at a family meeting or other gathering.

- "Inspiration" software that teaches mapping and webbed connections is very graphic and useful for making connections and cementing memory. It can be introduced in elementary school.

- Tapping out new vocabulary words or number facts to a rhythm, or even pacing back and forth while a child recites is helpful.

- Talk through the steps of math problems. Put number facts to music. Sing them to your favorite tune or make up a tune.

- Use mnemonics. These are shorts cuts we use to store, then later retrieve basic facts or rules. Examples are: HOMES for the names of the Great Lakes (Huron, Ontario, Michigan, Erie, and Superior) or "Thirty Days Has September, April, June and November." Teach the old standards, but also invent new ones when there is a new list that must be memorized.

- Visualize spelling or vocabulary words. Close your eyes and try to see them. Write them in the air. Whisper them under your breath. Write spelling words by tracing them in rice or flour on a paper plate; or use shaving cream or whipped cream to practice letters or words.

- Use flash cards. Give lots of adulation for success.

Fun games can prepare kids of any age for the memory challenges in school. You can sneak some in, and they won't even know they're doing mental gymnastics:

- Mental Travel: Close your eyes. In your mind's eye, travel through your bedroom or kitchen or garage. List as many things you can see that are brown or shiny or red.

- Recall the Objects: Collect ten objects. Put them on a tray. Cover with a cloth. Gather two or three family members and pull back the cloth. Give them twenty seconds to study them. Then cover them up and ask them to list all that they can remember. (Try this at a family meeting sometime.)

- Make Associations: Throw out a word. Kids need to rattle off as many things that they can remember that connect to this word. They can be silly or not. For example, if the word is green, they can say frog, spinach, envy or Bob Green, your neighbor.

- Interesting Facts: Grab hold of an almanac or Guinness Book, or "Amazing Facts for Kids." Recite a section. Close the book. See how many they can remember.
- Board games such as "Concentration," "Clue," and "Memory" build capacity.

For Older students:

- Teach them to chunk. Chunking involves recalling a long list of numbers or items by grouping the items into smaller segments. For example, instead of trying to remember a list of ten numbers, (most people can only remember seven), treat the list as you would a telephone number. Instead of 6243290158, chunk the first three digits into a three digit group—624, as in an area code. Then a three digit chunk: 329; then a four digit chunk: 0158. This is far more effective than trying to remember ten digits at once. Chess players commonly chunk positions on the board to remember them.
- Encourage students to work with peers. Cull out key concepts. Talk about them. Fool around with ideas. Pull them apart. Create analogies and invent mnemonics together. Draw pictures, diagrams, and maps together.
- When studying, teach them to scan the heading, skim the whole chapter before they read it. Get a sense of the whole. Later, underline the important points; summarize key concepts. Write them down. Talk about key points to yourself. Memorize these first. Jot down your insights.
- Encourage students to ask themselves: What is the big picture behind this content? Why is it important and why do I need to know this? How does it relate to what I already know?
- When trying to learn a procedure, have students walk through the steps in their minds. Talk them out. Review the steps just before they need them.

- Doodle. Research shows that adults who doodle during lectures retain more of the lecture than those who do not doodle. The same has not been tested in young people, but may have the same effect. (But students should check with the teacher first. Some may not have heard of this recent research and may object.)

Note to the Reader: I realize this is a lot of content for you. But remember, these lists are intended to be resources used on an as-needed basis. With sticky notes mark the ones that apply to your child's level, and return to them as you wish. Or break off a piece under a heading that catches your eye, and just work on that one piece. At any rate, don't try to practice more than one or two skills at a time. Remember the balance. Work. Rest. Work. Rest. That's the pace that works well under any circumstances.

◆ ◆ ◆

Strategy 30:

Creative Thinking

The ticket to tomorrow's success is the ability to innovate.

We've already discussed the value of helping children to make connections. Steve Jobs would agree. He once said "Creativity is just connecting things," and certainly went far in demonstrating that himself. Cognitive neuroscientist, Adele Diamond, says the essence of creativity is to be able to disassemble and recombine elements in new ways.

Creativity means different things to different people. Many believe creativity implies the invention or the origination of something new, with implications of freedom of thought, release from strictures, stretching beyond the margins, an expression of the spirit, free wheeling responses, and/or the ability to put one's unique mark on the world.

Author, Josh Lehrer in his 2012 Book, *Imagine*, says that creativity is not a superpower—that anyone can be creative, but we need practice. Daydreaming is a productive skill, according to Lehrer, and if it were up to him, "we'd teach kids how to effectively mind-wander in school." Schools value creativity, but don't always encourage it. Teaching and encouraging "creativity," can be a complicated affair. There's always the fear that it can lead to unruly behavior. In fact, Lehrer himself said, "he wouldn't have wanted to be one of Bob Dylan's teachers." Creativity is not counted on most tests, and frankly, most teachers simply don't know a lot about teaching it—if indeed it can be taught. Therefore, most don't bother. That doesn't mean parents can't try to encourage it.

Some of the strategies we've already discussed may help foster creativity from the earliest years with a child: spending time on the floor with the baby—rolling around and engaging in make-believe: encouraging exploration—signaling "go for it:" reading and making up stories: creating new endings to stories or plays: and playing word games. All of these lay the groundwork for creativity, as do others. Stock up on markers, clay, pipe cleaners, and all kinds of craft materials. Use previously discussed strategies from the various domains complement creativity: not being too obsessive about neatness when using craft material; exposure to all forms of the arts; exercising; engaging the hands in a variety of activities; providing good nutrition and sound sleep; controlling anxiety and stress; fostering a non-authoritarian climate; celebrating the joy and awe around us; and simply having fun. All of these positively affect creativity.

Additionally, as they grow one may want to try some of these:

- Name all the things that come in pairs.
- How would you improve a bike, a shoe, a hat, a book-bag?
- What alternate uses can you think of for a brick, a pencil, a piece of masking tape, a popsicle stick?
- What number belongs to you? Why?
- If the answer is 52, what are the questions?
- List as many impossibilities as you can.
- Solve Mother Hubbard's problem.
- What happened when the cow jumped over the moon?

The internet, of course, has many more specific strategies and activities to draw from. As children get older make sure they continue to be exposed to the arts. Some may start to resist. Maybe they see themselves as jocks or techies or some other classification that is mutually exclusive to the arts. But don't let them fall prey to this distorted idea. Find a play, an art show or musical event that you think may fit their style and just take them along. Additionally:

- Be freewheeling in your own demeanor sometimes. To some, this may mean lightening up a bit. Maybe it's not your natural style, but everyone can benefit from a good joke or a divergent thought or action now and then.

- Share funny stories or news clippings at dinner time. Enjoy Mad-Libs with your youngsters, or bring home a copy of "The Onion," or a similar parody publication for your teen.

- Search for online creativity games and play a few. Look for videogames that have a creative component to them. Share a hearty laugh at some truly good TV humor now and then.

Brainstorming, too, has traditionally been used to loosen up one's thinking--to get the juices flowing. It's been the mainstay of many a gifted seminar, and even many a board room. Brainstorming asks participants to generate a lot of ideas very quickly—to tap into their subconscious minds and bring forth as many associations as they can. I recently watched a middle school class sitting in a circle and passing around a plain white lined index card, and the teacher said, "Make as many connections as possible"—literally a stream of consciousness activity. Then she asked, "What is it?" The associations flew:… "A sail, a fan, a race track, a fence, a polar bear in a blizzard, a tall white building. In rapid succession these and many other associations kept coming. One student bent the card, and curled it up—"a cigarette" he deemed, changing course. Others followed: "a Chinese handcuff, a telescope, a fat pen, a chunk of rope, a piece of chalk, a pipe," etc. Then another varied the shape, and called out, "it's a scoop" followed by other piggy-backers: a shovel, a ramp, a skate board half-pipe, a chute, a flexible chopping board, and so on. The analogies flowed—silly or zany, it didn't matter. Students were learning the art of the metaphor and the simile in a fun way. And the connections kept coming—who knows from where?

There were only four little rules: Be freewheeling. No repetitions. No criticism. And quantity matters. And they were honored. The students seemed energized. They seemed surprised and pleased with their production.

Brainstorming is used in the corporate world when there are hopes of developing new products or refining existing ones. It's also used to generate new ideas for solving organizational glitches. While some complain that brainstorming just makes people feel good and lacks rigor, the process still works for many, and it's simple enough for parents to use with their kids to generate connections, and show them that it's okay to be freewheeling sometimes. It is also a good way to have fun with them.

> It's been my observation that students gain a measure of confidence in their own creative abilities when they brainstorm. "Wow. Where did all those ideas come from? I didn't know I had it in me!"

Author, Josh Lehrer reminds us wisely, to never push the envelope. Creativity cannot be forced. When you think you are stuck—"just relax," he says. Turn away from the project. Do something mindless. Take a hot shower. Listen to music. Go for a run. Take a nap. When your mind feels freed up, it will usually reward you with a creative solution. This is good advice for children as well as adults.

In her 2011 book, *Spark: How Creativity Works*, author, Julie Burstein shares interviews with 36 accomplished creative artists from various fields, and the "love" of each shines through. (This is reminiscent of Bloom's super-achievers, who first fell in love with their field, before pushing themselves to excel.) Frequently the "love" precedes the expression of creativity. For example, professional cellist, Yo-Yo Ma, told Burstein about "each day reacquainting himself with his beautiful Montagnana cello, made in Venice in 1733, which he nicknamed Petunia." The love shone through.

Sleep is a particularly interesting correlative to creativity. The literature is rich with examples of people who prime themselves for creating a song, a story, or solving a problem through sleep. They bring the creative challenge to the fore of their consciousness (even though they have no solution) right before they go to sleep. Then they let go and doze off. When they awake, "Voila." They discover the idea has come to them. Even Albert Einstein sang the praises of "priming" to break through that invisible barrier to creative problem solving. He used it often.

Older children have a tendency to lose their creative abilities. Parents may need to help coax them out of too much compliance, and adherence to rules. To some students, rote memory in order to attain high grades is more important than fresh thinking. But ironically, the very same teachers they are aiming to please, are looking for that "out of the box thought." And those students who can do that, will earn the extra points and set themselves apart. Some of the most advanced questions on the SAT's and ACT's probe for these abilities, too.

Reward your child for taking chances. Even for failing, sometimes. And remember to praise the "effort," not always the outcome.

No one knows what creative potential abides within a child. Some of those dormant genes are just dying for someone to tap on their doors. Stimulate them. Flip those switches. Turn those knobs. Parents can come to the rescue and release those anxious endorphins!

◆ ◆ ◆

Strategy 31:

Paying Attention

I wish I knew then what I know now. "My kids are half grown," one parent said, "and I'm just now finding out how powerful something as simple as 'paying attention' can be. And how it can help build a brain."

Yes, we want our children to be freewheeling—but not all the time. There are times when we want them to pay attention. But then again, it's understandable that they sometimes do not. After all, most of us have minds that wander, too. It's frustrating—yes, but it's not altogether a bad thing.

Alice wandered in Wonderland. So did Dorothy in Oz. Odysseus did. As did Huck Finn and Siddhartha and Alexander the Great. And each of them had wonderful adventures and exciting outcomes, didn't they? So wandering can pay off big sometimes. But we know that if done to excess, it can also stymie growth and get one into a lot of hot water.

Consider the kid I saw chasing butterflies in the outfield when he was supposed to be catching the ball. Or the little girl banging her mom's purse on the church pew while the pastor tried to deliver a homily. They were in for trouble.

So it's best to teach children to limit their mental wanderings. To control their minds. To know when and how to pay attention to the tasks at hand.

Kids need to know this for more reasons than just staying out of trouble. Paying attention sculpts the brain, and disciplines the mind. According to a January, 2012 article in the *Daily Beast* by science reporter Sharon Begley, "Neuroscientists have shown over and over that attention is the 'sine que non' of learning and thus of boosting intelligence. It is 'almost magical' in its ability to physically alter the brain and enlarge functional circuits... one of the strongest findings in neuroplasticity."

Who knew? To most of us, Mom's scolding to "pay attention" was just a ploy to keep the kids in line—just something that parents were supposed to do!

> I doubt if mom knew what researchers now know: that paying attention boosts one's processing speed, expands and creates functional networks, strengthens synapses and enhances the memory.

She just nagged: "Pay attention!"

"Paying attention" is alternately referred to and overlaps with focusing, concentrating, self-regulating, and/or exercising self control. (Many strategies related to self-control were discussed under Strategy Eighteen, for example and these build attention skills as well.)

For older children, some examples of tasks that enhance the ability to pay attention are:

- Playing a musical instrument
- Learning a new language
- Learning a new dance
- Playing chess
- Meditation
- Solving difficult math problems
- Writing poems, stories and songs
- Committing passages and verses to memory
- Making and editing movies
- Mastering certain videogames—especially those that involve switching attention quickly from one activity to another, and ascending levels of rigor

Though we don't ordinarily think of these as accelerating mental power, some non-academic activities that require meticulous attention to detail can offer wonderful benefits. Examples would be: sculpture, painting, woodworking, stenciling, calligraphy, knitting, model making and a host of other arts and crafts. Even manual tasks such as grooming and caring for pets, housekeeping, polishing silverware, arranging flowers, cooking and baking, planting, gardening, etc. should not be counted out as well. Any task that demands attention builds circuitry.

A preschool program, "Tools of the Mind," shows particular promise for encouraging three and four years olds to acquire organizational skills and to learn to pay attention. Much of the preschoolers' day in that program is given over to planning, concentrating and reporting out on their goals, and in refining and focusing on their work. In essence, they learn much about "paying attention." Studies of students in the program showed significant growth in self control and academic improvement compared to a control group who did not participate in the study.

For slightly older students, some games and activities help build attention skills, such as:

- Simon Says
- Twenty Questions
- I Spy
- Red Light-Green Light
- Musical chairs
- Any game with rules
- Jigsaw puzzles
- Solving riddles
- Manipulative puzzles such as Rubik's Cube and other hand-held brainteasers

In humans of any age, activities that are novel, challenging, and emotionally powerful, not only support memorization, they also assist one who is trying to "pay attention"; so too, are activities that are voluntary, repetitious and involve switching (such as a sudden change to another mode as is often required in some videogames).

Would you have thought that these simple acts of paying attention could be so magical—that they could physically alter the brain and enlarge functional circuits and help build up the prefrontal cortex? Well, they do.

So go on. Nag. Feel no guilt. Exercise your natural authority. Say what you need to say: " Practice your piano." "Pick up your clothes." "Do your number facts." "Study those vocabulary words... And when you're finished—an only then—you may go outside and practice your lay-ups."

Yes, it's dirty work. But, somebody has to do it. And you're it, Mom and Dad.

◆ ◆ ◆

Strategy 32:

Language

Laying on the language has always been one of the more easy ways to stimulate a child. Still is.

Lay it on. Talking and reading to children—especially early in life, increases IQ. According to psychologist and author, John Medina, by age three, kids who were talked to regularly by their parents (a group he called the talkative group) had IQ scores significantly higher than those kids whose parents talked to them the least (whom he called the taciturn group).

This jives with my observations of parents of successful students. They were mostly a very chatty group—with lots of opinions—and they rarely held back. They listened well and encouraged children to express their own opinions. I suspect all this had a substantial influence on their children's high verbal scores. In fact, one parent said that life with her meant one long never-ending conversation. And presumably it wasn't a one-way conversation.

Language is both receptive and expressive. Sometimes we listen and sometimes we speak. We need both.

- Listen. Listen with your head and your heart, and your whole being. Pick up all their cues. Respond and reciprocate. This is what researchers now tell us is critical—even more important than what we say to our children. From the first moments of your child's life, listen, respond, and reciprocate. Be emotionally, and psychologically as well as physically present for them.

- Communicate verbally. Typically, communication flows naturally and informally. Even when Mom is pregnant, she and Dad can still talk to the baby. ("I'm playing my new CD now, Darling. How do you like it? Do you want to give me a little kick to let me know?") Then later as the child grows and parent and child move about the community, communication is sustained—lots of conversation around routines, trips to the market, playing games, singing songs, cooking, exploring nature, counting and measuring objects together, etc. Learning and language development occur naturally and ongoing.

- Play. Play enhances early language, too. You generally talk while you are coloring or playing with water, strings, sand, clay, or building blocks, Legos, puzzles, model cars, planes, and kits, or following simple instructions for assembling articles, taking apart and putting together toys and clocks, etc. Language is part of all the activities that are embedded in a child's day. When you get involved, the words just flow.

- Organize time around games. Games will encourage language development—matching games, rhyming games, shape shorting games, treasure hunts and assembling puzzles for starters. Later card and board games, chess, electronic and videogames; games like "I Spy," "Ghost," and "twenty questions, riddles, and brain teasers, "Trivial Pursuit," "Pictionary," "Boggle," "Scrabble," and many online and videogames generally involve language. Certain genes are associated with verbal potential. Titillate them.

- Snuggle. Cuddle up when you read to your baby or preschooler. Make it a warm and intimate experience. You want them to associate reading and books with that warmth. Parents should continue reading to children when they are older. An inspirational or exciting piece from an editorial or a magazine can be shared at dinner to children of any age. Make words special. Share ones that delight you for some reason or another. Look challenging ones up together in the dictionary. Use a thesaurus to extend meanings. Sharing literacy in any form helps establish an intellectual climate in the home.

Some parents of very high achievers admitted to reading to their preschoolers up to three or four hours per day—usually broken into segments. I'm not saying that this should be the norm—only what I have been told was the norm for some families. And this is fine if the child is fully interested and engrossed. But watch out for signs of fatigue, for too much of a good thing can actually be detrimental. Take your cues from the child.

Reading habits have changed radically in past years. Today many young readers have their own iPads, Kindles, Nooks or other electronic readers, which is great, if students are also reading actual books. But sometimes too much of their online time involves reading of text messages, Facebook or blogs. These do not equate to the value of a good book for ideas are seldom sustained in online text. They are often bits and pieces of information—chopped and pressed—short on depth and wisdom. Seldom do these blurbs force a student to grapple with new ideas. So don't let them wriggle out of good reading. There is no substitute for great literature.

Here are some further general recommendations from parents and the literacy experts:

- Talk to the baby while you are still pregnant. Sing to him. (Some studies indicate that the fetus can hear the mother's voice and sense her mood.)

- After the baby is born, talk to him in a high-pitched voice, and speak slowly. This is sometimes called "parentese." It is generally helpful. Read to your child every day. Read interactively. "Where's the puppy? Yes. That's the puppy. Right there. Now where is the cat?" Make reading time fun.

- Involve your child when you read, by letting him point to the pictures and turn the page.

- Model reading. Let your children see you reading every day. Like joy, it's contagious.

- Read fiction. Non-fiction. Prose. Poetry. Biographies. Stories related to his personal interests. Read him some of everything and anything.

- Have small children dictate stories. Create a book. Then read them back.

- Do shared reading with young children. You read some. Then he reads some.

- Share highlights from your favorite readings at family dinners or family meetings. Rotate the reader. Make it a special honor.

- Give books as gifts. Ask for books as gifts.

- Play with words. Crossword puzzles, anagrams, Scrabble, Boggle, and Bananagrams, UpWords. Charades. Twenty Questions, and many other games involve word fun. Share jokes, puns, riddles, tongue twisters.

- Ask kids to summarize a movie, a book, a TV show, a basketball game, a party, any event after the fact.

- Summarize what you've read for a child.

- Keep a reading journal—a list of books read with comments; also a list of books you'd like to read. Share with your middle or high schooler.

- Check out "Goodreads" online for electronic tracking of your reading.

- Make a habit of using the dictionary and thesaurus. Delight in new words.

- Encourage storytelling. Create alternate endings to favorite stories.

- Limit time for videogames and TV. Declare a family reading time.

- Join or create a book club. Start or join Junior Great Books Club at your child's school.

- Insist on hand-written thank you notes.

- Write letters to the editors of papers, congressmen, celebrities, the Better Business Bureau, even the President when you find an issue that needs attention.

- Always bring a book or two along on vacation.

Again, pick and choose from these lists those that fit your situation and your child's needs and strengths.

♦ ♦ ♦

Strategy 33:

Simple Conversations

Much of parenting doesn't have to be "rocket science." These are plenty of easy ways to encourage children to work hard put and forth effort. "Simple conversations" rank up there.

Simple conversations give children a reason to learn content. And a good chunk of those occur during ordinary moments that stretch out over the years. Lessons get taught. Values are shared. Relationships grow deeper, and layers of language accrete.

Here are examples of simple conversations that parent shared around the theme of "hard work," and how they encouraged them to do it:

1. "I tell my kids stories. Lots of stories. True stories. Simple stories. They love to hear them—especially the ones about the 'olden days.' For example, I'll say, 'Your grandfather came to this country as a penniless immigrant. He worked eighteen to twenty hours a day in his shop in the garment district. (It was true, by the way). The family was very poor then. But gradually, through his hard work and perseverance, we were able to move out of poverty. Now we live in a nice house. And you and your brother get to go to a good school.' They listen, and I think because it's true, it makes an impression."

2. "We watch the biography channel together. Then afterwards we talk about some of those great figures in history. They've all

overcome hurdles and the kids get that. The heroes have learned to work things through. It's matters that it's from someone other than the parents—though we get a chance to put our 'two cents' in. The media, the libraries, the internet are all filled with stories of self-made people who bootstrapped themselves, so I would encourage other parents to draw on all those resources."

3. "Sometimes I use examples of people we know. I'll say, 'Mr. Smith (our neighbor) loves his job as CEO. He told me he gets real pleasure from using his mind and working with all different kinds of people. He had to study very hard and put in many long hours to learn his business, but it's really paid off. That's the kind of determination it takes.'"

4. "I use conversations to help my children solve problems when they hit a hurdle. I try not to solve the problems for them, but ask them a lot of questions to help them figure things out for themselves. We use the classic John Dewey problem solving model. It seems to help." (See Strategy Twenty-Two.)

5. "I remind my kids that the pleasure of effort comes from stretching yourself—running, playing basketball, doing puzzles, reading, making models, and learning about new ideas. They've got to learn to stretch. We set limits on all activities that do not lead to substantive work. This is how I put it: 'I cannot let you sit in front of a TV screen all day. It will turn your mind to mush. So it's just not going to happen in our house. And I draw the line because I love you, and I want you to do well. Not because I'm mean.'"

6. "Some of our most important conversations have been about failures: 'No one wins all the time… When you fall down, get up and try again. Some of life's greatest lessons come out of our failures. Look at Steve Jobs. That's what happened to him and so many others. But you don't have to go that far. Look at Uncle Louey. He failed at a couple of businesses before this one… But he picked himself up. Now he's making a mint.'"

7. "Periodically, I remind them that school is their job. Just as their mother has a job, and I have a job, so they, too, have a job. And their job is called, 'school.' A main responsibility is to that job. They must take their schoolwork seriously. You can't assume kids make that connection. You have to talk to them about it."

8. "We dream together a lot. I think it's important to look toward the future. We talk about goals and career possibilities. We entertain wild outcomes. I tag onto current events a lot—whatever's in the news: 'I wonder what it would be like to be the first person to go to Mars, or bring all warring nations to the peace table—or to break an Olympic record?' It can set them on fire—at least for awhile. Sure circumstances can change. And so will some plans. But first you have to give them their dreams. Big dreams. And if things change, … oh well, we'll cross that bridge… As they grow, I let them know that is okay, too."

◆　◆　◆

Strategy 34:

Organizational Skills

*Organized students sometimes run rings around
disorganized peers of much higher ability.
It's the old "tortoise and the hare."*

Organizational skills definitely bestow an advantage. Billy, a fifth grader, was such an example. He was busy—busy—always busy. Some thought he was ADHD, but I disagreed. To me, he was just a bundle of energy—but without the disorganization that typically characterized ADHD children. He did not have a super high I.Q. He often outstripped his more talented classmates when it came to getting the work done. When some kids reacted with dread at the announcement of the upcoming science fair, Billy gave a loud, "YES," jabbing the air with of a tightened fist. He rolled up his sleeves and got to work, then he murmured, "first, we'll pick a topic… Then we'll narrow a goal. Then we'll outline a timeline." He knew how to organize the project before I could give instructions. He made lists. He sketched his plans, and even made a flow chart, with all the savvy of a CEO. I didn't need to review the steps numerous times as I did with some of the others. Billy just knew what steps to take, and in what order. Billy went on to take first prize in the science fair and eventually to become the high school valedictorian.

I asked Billy's mom about his extraordinary sense of organization that gave him an edge. "Yes. We put a big premium on organizational skills in our house," she said. "You've heard of the saying: 'Success is one percent inspiration and ninety-nine percent perspiration?' Well, that's us."

Later, she elaborated: "We started him early. As a toddler, we sorted clothes, money, books, toys, 'junk,' kitchen utensils,— anything to get him familiar with common attributes, and to help him make connections. Later we sorted food in the pantry. I made him my assistant. We sorted laundry, tools, and household items. It became a game. As he grew, we outlined steps we needed to take. We talked aloud about the goal and the sequence and details needed to achieve it. We made lists. We always started big projects with a meeting to review the scope and how to bear down on the project. I'd say, 'Now Billy this is going to be hard, but we can do it.' We'd celebrate when we were done. We'd rate the work—even award gold stars or stickers for jobs well-done."

One pre-school program, "Tools of the Mind," previously mentioned, encourages and trains three and four year olds to organize their time and materials, and studies have shown remarkable results. Students plan their mornings by drawing pictures or telling the teacher what they intend to do with a block of time. "I'll play firehouse, or zoo, or dress up for the kings' ball," they may say. Then they carry it out, later reporting how things have gone. They also do buddy reading and critique their independent work with a classmate. (They may ask, "How does my letter 'B' compare with the teacher's letter "B?") Three and four year olds learn very early on how to structure their time and work and how to hold themselves accountability. They are not free to just ramble. Studies show that children in the "Tools of the Mind" program are not only more organized, but have shown improvement in working memory, flexible thinking, and impulse control. Other programs such as the Montessori Method, also emphasize organization at an early age, and studies have shown that those students can internalize similar skills at an early age.

For older children:

- Encourage collections such as rocks, cancelled stamps, quarters from the various states and other coins. This requires sorting, classification, etc.

- Keep a family calendar to coordinate activities and avoid conflicts.

- Make lists and check off tasks as they are accomplished.

- Use a planner to organize assignments and important papers.

- Provide a place to study. A kitchen counter can be as useful as a desk—especially if parents are nearby to help with homework.

- Establish a homework routine.

- Cook together. Following directions, sorting and measuring ingredients and managing time can be fun and instructive.

- Model good organization yourself. Never use terms such as "I'm not an organized person," or "organization is not in our genes." Instead, tout the advantages of being organized such as the time-savings for not having to look for misplaced items, etc.
- Reward for jobs that are well-done.
- If your child's school does not offer "Study Skills" refer to appendix for some useful sites under "Resources."

♦ ♦ ♦

Strategy 35:

Technology

Could any bag be more mixed than technology?
One minute we're riding its wave and singing
its praises, the next cursing its influence.

According to the Kaiser Family Research, the average kid spends approximately 7.5 hours a day in front of a blinking screen. That's more time than they spend in school. Many children are also multitasking—watching TV while they text with their friends, etc, so their total hours of combined streaming may be as high as 11 hours a day. Technology can be a great blessing or a regrettable time-waster.

> We should ask, "How did all this technology sneak up on us? Who and what is molding our children? Can we allow it? Should we allow it? Will we allow it?" If the answer is "yes," what forms should this take? That is for you to decide; but in all cases, much oversight is in order, and we can only expect that the parental role will increase in this respect over time.

First, let it be said that technology is wonderful in many ways—a huge blessing that has simplified and enhanced our lives immeasurably. It allows us to communicate, research, and enjoy the arts and life with more ease that we ever imagined. Education has become more personalized and social networks are enhanced. Many middle and high schools are introducing more "blended learning," (blending online courses with traditional face-to-face coursework), thereby making more effective use of instructional time. There is no doubt that children need to hone their computer skills to succeed in school today, but parental oversight at home is essential, too.

Studies show that the excessive use of technology has been linked to poor decision-making, memory loss, attention disorders, and social maladjustment in some children. Technology use can be addictive and needs to be constrained. Parents must plan a prominent role in oversight. It's very easy to be overwhelmed and to want to say, "I can't keep up", and turn a blind eye. But this is one of the worst things parents can do. It's important to keep current as best one can.

Some pitfalls of this high-tech world, such as texting while driving, or being vulnerable to online predators, are highlighted in the media, but some threats are less well-disseminated. For example, parents should know that some studies show that excessive use of technology rewires young brains—especially those of multi-taskers, who pay more attention to the "ping" of the latest message coming in, than the main project at hand. By constantly going back and forth between "projects," answering the phone, watching TV, listening to music, composing and reading text messages, etc., they fail to sustain concentration and focus. It is believed that the pattern and rhythm of the "fits and starts" may be reprogramming the brain, making it more difficult to perform more substantive subsequent tasks, such as reading a book, or sustaining a single idea in depth. Unrestricted use is not a good idea.

Like computers, television is another mixed blessing. Yes, there are many fine entertaining and educational programs on TV. But if we could factor out the inane ones, and the inappropriate ads, trying to sell them junk foods and silly products that they don't need (but don't know they don't need), it wouldn't be so bad. Short of posing opportunities for critical thinking and discernment skills, we should be asking, WHY?

Violence is yet another ongoing major concern—both on television and with videogames. According to the American Academy of Pediatrics, by age 18, the average child in America will have viewed 200,000 acts of violence on television alone. One has to wonder what all these shootings are doing to the children's subconscious minds.

Experts have raised the question of children and empathy. Will students who spend so much time with technology be able to sustain empathy in relationships when so many relationships are becoming virtual?

Academically, will students be able to cull the big picture when their world is so fragmented? Will their understanding of nature be limited to what they have learned virtually? Will they care? It will be years before we truly know technology's long term effects.

I do not intend to paint an unduly bleak picture of technology when we all know of its many benefits. It's just that we don't know the costs of the tradeoffs. The unrestricted use of technology is not a good idea. Students need balance in their lives. And parents need to stay on top of technology, and its effects on the children. It is one of the great challenges of our day. Parents need to make an effort to stay abreast of all aspects of technology in our children's lives, and they need to demand to be included in the dialogue regarding products as markets expand. Ask yourself: "What will be my stand?"

Meanwhile, at home, some strict guidelines should be put in place:

- Limit TV and videogames. (While both have academic value, but also have negative consequences.) Seek balance.

- Discuss rules for appropriate use of computers.

- Install Internet filtering and monitoring software. (Some smart kids can get around these. If you have doubts or questions, ask for a consult with your school's technology coordinator.)

- Talk to your children about Internet safety. Caution them about cyber-bullying and Internet predators. Let them know the proper responses.

- Allow younger children to use the computer only in a family common area.

- If you allow older children to use computers in their bedroom, insist that their doors be open.

- Know what websites you child is visiting. Check for reviews of websites on *CMCH.tv* or at: *www.commonsensemedia.org*.

- Let them know that you will check on their browsing histories and look into any sites you do not understand. (This is not an intrusion of their privacy—even for older students. Even if they are eighteen, as long as they are living in your house and you are paying the bills, you get to make the rules. These issues are too important for parents to be detached or wishy-washy. Maintain control.)

- Discuss plagiarism and the value of intellectual property with them. Let them know it is not acceptable to cut and paste, and claim content as their own. Proper citations are always essential. Get them in the habit early.

- Ban all electronics at dinnertime. (That time is too precious.)

- Consider setting a turn-off time, such as 9:30 PM, when all technology goes off. No exceptions.

In some families, rules are typed out and posted. Others use contracts, which the children sign, and to which they are held accountable. Even with all that, ongoing vigilance is still necessary. Let them help explain what you don't know, but reiterate, "You are still the boss."

Explain that if your stance seems strict, it's because you love them and care about them, and want them to be healthy and safe. It bears repeating that students need balance in their lives—and excessive use of technology increasingly interferes with that. So pull out your imaginary PACT-o-meter from time to time, and tell the kids you want to "talk about the Whole You." Involve your child in an assessment if you feel he's old enough to understand:

Physical: Is sleep being compromised by blinking screens or sounds of phones going off in the night? Are eating habits being compromised by ads for fast food and junk food? Is everyone getting enough exercise? Fresh air? Sunshine? Explain that virtual experiences will never compare to real ones. Electronic images pale compared to what we perceive and receive through our magnificent senses.

Affective: Are real flesh and blood relationships being affected? (Some kids are known to text each other, even when they are both in the same room.) Huh? Is the child spending too much time alone in front of the screens—lacking face-to-face encounters? Not exercising his social skills?

Cognitive: Is technology gobbling up time with low level activities? (It's easier to spend time collecting and compiling lots of data versus thinking deeply about dilemmas or weighing decisions, drawing conclusions, or generating creative solutions.) Critical and creative thinking require an investment of one's "real time," versus time taken up with mindless applications which can be pure time-wasters.

Transcendence: Is time for reflection being crowded out by gadgets? (They are no substitute.) Is there ample time to savor nature, art, and music? Do avatars and virtual realities take their proper place behind the amazing entity known as the human spirit? Are decisions made on the basis of retrieved bits of information—or does one put holistic intuition and hunches into the mix sometimes?

Network with other parents. Talk to your school's technology coordinator about the best ways to use technology and reduce dangers. Make it your business to keep up as best you can and to insure your children live progressive but well-balanced live.

◆　◆　◆

Strategy 36:

Know the System

What good are all the pains you've taken with your child, if the school culture is a foreign element? Learn the system. Know its rhythm. Play it like a violin.

Consider this: You've taken pains to groom him since birth, but so have all the others. Some parents know all the little fine points about maneuvering within the system but others do not. Few talk about these, so you just have to pick them up. Don't let the child lose an edge because you're out-of-touch with the school culture. That culture wields a strong influence, and could make a difference. To maximize your child's school experience, you've got to get in synch and stay in synch. Every level has its idiosyncrasies, which you should know about to give your child the advantage. Keep up to speed. Know what is going on. Stay on top. Make yourself part of the action, but don't make a pest of yourself. Much more could be said here—particularly by a former administrator, but I'll spare you. Here are some highlights gleaned from many perspectives—parents, teachers and administrators.

- Pick the best possible school district or private school that you can afford. (Compare them online.) The culture permeates much of what your child will experience, and can determine how high the bar is set. (But if you don't have a choice, and the district where you live isn't the greatest, don't worry. There are smart kids and caring teachers everywhere. Just seek them out.)

- Find your own Wonder Parents—veterans of the school— those who have preceded you—who seem to know everyone and everything. Invite them to lunch. Inquire about the school culture. What's the most important thing to know about Washington Elementary? What are the "can't miss" events? How do you get your kids ready for the transition to middle school? Who are the "helpers" on the faculty? What's the best way to approach the principal?

- Get involved. Be a helper. Consider being a homeroom parent at the elementary level, or volunteering to chaperone events at the upper grades. (But check with your high school student first before chaperoning. Some will not appreciate it.)

- Volunteer for most key events. Find out what are the big ones—it may be the May Fair, the annual spaghetti dinner, field day, or some other "must be there event."

- Be visible around the school—but not too much. Join the PTA. Consider running for office if you have the time and have learned the ropes.

- Introduce yourself to the school secretary, the crossing guard, the bus driver. Know them by name. Remember each with a little treat or a small plant at the holidays.

- Know the curriculum. Ask to see the manuals. Check to see if they are online, first.

- Consider purchasing a copy of "What Every First Grader Needs to Know," What Every Second Grader Needs to Know, etc. as it pertains to your child's level. These are sold online and in most book stores. (Core Knowledge Series.) Be sure you child is not being shortchanged.

- Study the district and school documents—handbooks and policy manuals. They contain some critical information. Most are now online. Know the rules and abide by them.

- Ask about grouping practices. (Request a meeting with a guidance counselor—or principal for this one.) If your child does not meet the criteria for a challenging group, but you are convinced she is capable of doing the work, consider tutoring if you can afford it. Ask for a list of recommended tutors. Talk frankly and respectfully about the possibility of a re-test to move up to the higher group if your child eventually meets the criteria.

- If you child shows interest and promise in a special area, such as art or music, ask about the possibility of extra tutoring by a faculty member after school hours.

- As they go up the grades, familiarize yourself with the course sequences and prerequisites.

- Algebra and Geometry are particularly important. They are called "gateway courses," because they are necessary to qualify for higher level courses. Even if your child is headed for a technical education, he could be shut out if he is not competent in those courses. Prioritize support in these areas.

- If the school does not offer a separate study skills course, or a test-prep mini-course (which is sometimes embedded in an English course) you may want to consider one outside of school. Huntingdon and Sylvan Learning Centers, etc. offer these. If not, look for a good book on the topic, or online study skills resources.

- If your child is strong in math, science, technology or the humanities, inquire about opportunities to participate in the Intel, or Siemens-Westinghouse, or Junior Science and Humanities Symposia.

- Check the Kahn Academy online for tutorials to supplement content areas, if the current teacher is not getting through to your student.

- Befriend a guidance counselor or similar "power person,"—the school librarian, department head, assistant principal, coach, athletic director, etc.—someone you can relate to. Invite them into your home. Wine and dine them. Be low key, and don't ask too many questions at first. Eventually, you may need specific information about criteria for scholarships, special programs, etc, and this will set you apart, because now they know you. When you call, hopefully they will connect you to the proper resources.

- If you don't understand the class rank system, find someone who can explain it to you—early on. Make sure you child understands this, too. No one likes surprises.

- Pick courses that are the best match to the child's strengths and interests. Don't let her drift into courses because her friends are in them, or just "fit neatly into the schedule." (When in doubt, refer to that journal you started when they were a baby. You know, the one with the tweed cover.)

- Always be respectful, but when necessary, be assertive— not aggressive, but assertive. Don't let the schools intimidate you.

Sound bossy? Too much chutzpah? Maybe. But this is what involved parents do.

Let your college bound kids know that they, too, can't be shy. Show them how it's done. Say, "Soon you'll be in college and on your own. You'll need to find your way—pick your own courses—deal with the system. We can't be thin-skinned. We have to be on it."

Chapter 7:
The Transcendent Domain

INTRODUCTION:

Many believe that raising a child to be a good person is more important than raising a super achiever.

There is no denying that some of topics we've already discussed have a transcendent element to them—bonding and falling in love with the baby, for example—or visualization of goals, making connections, creating, innovating, etc. But to some the transcendent, (like the affective) is a little bit murky. They're not quite sure what it encompasses, nor what to do about it.

You, yourself, may ask: What is Transcendence? Why is it important? How does one experience it? How do I recognize and encourage it in my child?

Transcendence means different things to different people.

Webster defines transcendence as a state "exceeding usual limits; surpassing; extending or lying beyond the limits of ordinary experience." For many of us, it's a stretch—something a little beyond our reach and hard to grasp.

Parents view transcendence through a variety of lenses. They also use a plethora of terms to describe it:

Faith

Religion

Spirituality

Nature

The Arts

Flow

Service to others

Intuition

Clarity of vision

Mindfulness and Meditation

An inner voice

Energy

Harmony

Rapture

Synchronicity

A higher plane

Connectedness with the universe, to name just a few.

Though transcendence and the spiritual areas are ordinarily not brought up in public schools, parents still weigh in. Here are a few things they said:

- "It's an essential ingredient to the well-being of the Whole Child."
- "Transcendence and spirituality add meaning to one's life,"
- "It refines the child. Transcendence helps develop moral and ethical competence,"
- "We're all born with the seeds of the spiritual within. They need to be cultivated."

If you're familiar with the work of the psychologist, Abraham Maslow, you've probably heard of his "Hierarchy of Needs." According to Maslow, a human's behavior mirrors his needs on an ascending scale. He must satisfy one level to move to the next.

First come physical needs (food, clothing, shelter); then safety, love, self-esteem, and self-actualization in that order. One moves up the continuum of functioning and thriving, only as the lower levels are satiated and satisfied. "Self actualization" has generally been viewed as the optimum level. But what most do not know is that in his 1971 uncompleted work, "The Farther Reaches of Human Nature," Maslow cited transcendence as the "very highest and most inclusive or holistic level of man's consciousness... "—a level beyond "self-actualization,"—the "apex of man's striving."

This is important, because Maslow is one of the most widely read and respected of American psychologists.

Maslow links self-actualization with "transcendence," citing these as the "being values... unconditional love, altruism, inner joy, a love of nature, the development of intuition, idealism, and a sense of wisdom." He also asserts that these values help develop creativity.

Throughout history, other great minds have also acclaimed the importance of transcendence, but as a concept, in America, it has not been particularly well-understood. China, India, Egypt and other ancient cultures, for example have long studied and fully acknowledged the role of transcendence in humans' well-being. This is not surprising, as these countries have a long tradition of taking a more holistic and comprehensive view of the universe.

But now these views are rapidly catching on in the West. Many major universities and medical schools now encompass departments of complementary, integrative or alternative medicine. They acknowledge transcendence and mind/body/ spirit connections, and apply them to healing, learning, and conservation of mental, physical, and emotional health. As we seek to raise children with balanced lives, we do well to stay abreast of these broader developing trends.

♦ ♦ ♦

Strategy 37:

Religion

That hour in church each week allows us to make sense of our lives' fragmented pieces. We're a very busy family, and Church adds balance.

Today many parents identify themselves as "spiritual," but not "religious. " Nonetheless, in America eighty-six percent of children are being raised to identify with a religious tradition. Worldwide about two-thirds of the people align themselves with a formal religion.

> According to clinical psychologist, Dr. Patrick Fagan, who analyzed over one hundred studies that traced various influences of religion on youth, students who attend a house of worship at least once a month get higher academic grades, have better behavior, less drug and alcohol involvement, less shoplifting, less runaways, less fighting and less theft.

While religion, per se, was not a topic parents typically initiated in the public school setting, comments still were made spontaneously—particularly in the context of the Whole Child.

- "Our time in the Synagogue each week is our time to connect what we're doing daily to something greater. It helps clarify our purpose on earth. "

- "I don't know about the others, but I need help... You know that expression—'It takes a village?' Well, Hillary got it right. I need the help of the village, including the village minister. So we're in church every week."

- "My son asked why we had to go to church every week. I told him: Even God needed rest on the seventh day. Why shouldn't we?"

When PACT discussions surfaced in parenting sessions, transcendence under various names was mentioned as a requisite component. Quite a few parents pointed to their religion as an anchor in their lives and an important part to their children's education. They believe it was essential to their total well-being. The Institute for American Values issued a statement that reverberated with those feelings. In their 2002 publication called, "Hardwired to Connect: The Scientific Case for Authoritative Communities," they state: "We are hardwired for other people and for moral meaning and openness to the transcendent. Meeting those basic needs for connection is essential to health and to human flourishing."

At times all children wonder and sometimes ask:

- Where did I come from?
- Where am I going?
- How can I get there?
- What happens after I die?

On a practical level, formalized religion provides a context to address those questions, without parents having to cast about awkwardly for answers they may not readily have. Parents say they are also grateful that faith provides coherence, meaning, and direction to their own lives, not only in coping with the daily grind, but with facing the intricacies of life and death issues.

Of course, it is possible to nurture a child's spiritual core outside the confines of a faith community. But judging by statistics, most find that participating in a faith tradition makes such nurturance much easier. With or without religion, some methods for encouraging and nurturing moral development are:

- Engaging children in discussions of moral quandaries and dilemmas.
- Modeling ethical behavior yourself.
- Sharing your values.
- Talking about issues of social justice.
- Engaging in social action and community service.
- Establishing family rituals, such as blessings at bedtime or grace before meals.
- Using exposure to holidays, and religious art and music in museums, and the media to fill in the lines related to the history and traditions of the respective religions.

Whether or not one joins a faith community, is of course, a personal decision. The freedom to do so or not, though, is something that affects the overall climate and context of one's environment. In a recent CSPAN presentation, writer/social commentator, Mark Steyn observed that the everyday life of people in countries that impose strictures on religion, such as Russia and China appears more difficult for the citizens than in those countries that enjoy total religious freedom, such as America. Many parents believe that those same effects trickle down and positively affect the well-being of children that are free to worship.

◆ ◆ ◆

Strategy 38:

The Arts

*In some families, the arts are akin to religion.
That is how they soar.*

Who can't remember some special moment from the past when we were carried away by a beautiful piece of music, transported by an uplifting book or film, or deeply moved by a piece of art? In such moments it seemed that we were temporarily removed from our earthly plane. There's no doubt that the arts are enriching and have the ability to do that. And sometimes the memory of those experiences can last a lifetime.

To many, the arts are the essence of transcendence. They are what inspire us to stretch and grow—to express ourselves—to become more than we are—or simply a reason to be.

Picasso said that "every child is an artist. The problem is how to remain an artist once we grow up." Continued and integrated transcendent experiences may help—experiences that are integrated with the physical, affective and cognitive dimensions of one's being. Early immersion and exposure to a variety of art forms can make deep impressions on young children, and thereafter may even become the foundation of their own striving.

Some families are more dedicated to providing artistic experiences and exposures than others. In fact, in some families, art is their central theme—their raison d'etre—and certainly synonymous with transcendence. Here are a few of the more memorable comments I have heard:

- "The arts say it all—they provide those special moments that can thrill and transport us. In a child, especially, I believe they inspire one to reach higher and higher."
- "The arts connect us to something greater than ourselves. They lift us up and resonate with our souls."
- "The arts are like some inner voice whispering in one's ear. One hopes one's child listens, and is, in some sense carried away. But I'll be happy if my child simply learns to enjoy and appreciate the arts."

The benefits of the arts are well documented in the literature.

Years of research show that art education is closely linked to academic achievement, social and emotional development, and civic engagement.

Studies also show that actual involvement in the arts is specifically associated with gains in mathematics, reading, critical and creative thinking, verbal skills and overall cognition. A 2005 report about the visual arts by the RAND corporation states that the art experience "can connect people more deeply to the world and open them to the new ways of seeing."

In his amazing book, *The World in Six Songs*, author Daniel Levitin tells us that through the arts we consciously and unconsciously integrate and make sense of our persona and respective worlds—internal and external. Music and art in general provide us with:

1. **Perspective:** the ability to think about our own thoughts and to realize that other people may have thoughts or beliefs that differ from our own.

2. **Representation:** the ability to think about things that aren't right there in front of us.

3. Rearrangement: the ability to combine, recombine, and impose hierarchical order on the elements in the world.

All children should be exposed to art. Their lives should not be allowed to slip out of balance, or become so crowded by gadgets or irrelevant minutiae, that they do not have time to resonate with the beauty around them and within their souls. In the worst case scenario, when those natural switches and knobs related to the arts are not activated, when those genes are not expressed, something withers. Innate potential is pruned away, and talent is wasted. The ideal would be for all children to play an instrument, and for all schools to provide a wide swath of visual arts, dance, drama and music appreciation. When districts slash arts programs they cut more than dollars. They cut vast amounts of human potential.

Whether practiced as a religion of its own, or in combination with formalized religion and other transcendent experiences, the arts invoke transcendence, cognition, social and emotional well-being and are an essential ingredient in the development of the well-rounded person. Parents do well to encourage the arts within their homes, their communities and their schools.

◆　◆　◆

Strategy 39:

Nature

You never know what mysteries nature will reveal to you. Show your child how to open their senses and celebrate nature.

I discovered there are quite a few parents who declare nature to be their personal religion. I distinctly remember opening an irritating note from one such parent, years ago when I was a principal:

"Dear Principal:
Our children will be out of school for the next three weeks, and I expect these to be excused absences."

She was telling me, not asking me for a legal excuse. The note was a fiat, not a request. I was essentially being informed that I would bend the rules for this family—and they did not expect to be challenged. As principal, I was used to getting requests for permission to miss school for vacations, but not ones with such a demanding tone. I was irked, but read on.

"I know this exceeds the district's policy for excused absences, but we believe we are entitled to a religious exemption. Nature is our religion, you know, so I'm sure that qualifies us." (Reading between the lines, she seemed to be saying, "Don't even think about denying me.") "We will be visiting Sequoia National Park in California to see the giant redwoods—nature's pure cathedral, and we deem this to be a legitimate excuse."

I won't go into all the legal red tape that was going through my mind about coding student's absences on state reports, nor the imaginary letters I could get from other parents who may catch wind of a loophole, and want the same treatment. But when I finally got down to the last line, I was sobered a bit:

"In the words of the great naturalist, John Muir: 'Everybody needs beauty as well as bread—places to play in and pray in, where nature may heal and give strength to body and soul.' Don't you agree?"

Yours truly.
Unconventional Parent

What could I say? "Exemption granted!"

Not only had the words moved me, but I knew the students were good kids, who rarely missed school, and could easily catch up. They would probably also greatly benefit from the trip. (And, as luck would have it, upon return the family appeared with an interesting array of souvenirs to share from their trip. They even volunteered to spearhead our upcoming Earth Day festivities. Clearly they practiced what they preached—their religion of nature.)

Another parent once reminded me that the famous architect, Frank Lloyd Wright said: "I believe in God. Only I spell it N-A-T-U-R-E." She gave me a card with those words written on it. (But that parent did not ask for any favors.)

Throughout history, Taoism, Wicca, parts of Buddhism and other religions of native/aboriginal peoples of the earth have deified nature and drawn from it powers. In varying degrees we all have transcendent reactions to the uplifting hand of Mother Nature.

We've all had our transcendent moments through nature. Which of us hasn't felt it by walking through a field of flowers, or viewing the setting sun, or discovering a rainbow, or walking out into the first quiet snowfall of the season. That "awesome wonder" fills us up and somehow leaves us a better person.

All children deserve such opportunities to commune with nature.

In *Meditation: The Complete Guide*, authors Patricia Monaghan and Eleanor G. Viereck, offer some simple suggestions to help parents and children commune with nature:

- Break out of your habit of starting your day with numbers and computers and look outside first. Open the door. Scan the sky. Check the weather. Take a deep breath of fresh air. Listen for any unusual sounds or sights—the wind, birds migrating, the appearance of new buds, changes in leaf colors, or the scent of some flowers in bloom. (You'll find some if you look.)

- Thank Providence aloud for the gift of the natural world.
- On the weekend, spend some extra time outside. Bring your child along with you. Take a leisurely stroll. Even if you live in a city, you will find plants, animals, and the sky to enjoy. Chances are your child will discover more than you. The younger the child, the more features of nature he will point out.
- Find a spot to sit quietly for awhile. Comment on the cycles of the seasons and anything else that strikes you. Again, express gratitude for nature's gifts.
- Plan to make a special mini-field trip to mark the change of seasons. Celebrate the first day of spring or fall—or any season or new month.

It goes without saying that visits to state and national parks and vacations in rural settings offer great rewards and opportunities for growth. But Mother Nature will welcome you anywhere—in your yard, on your street, or at a local arboretum or nature center.

> Spending time to commune with nature is a perfect foil to help balance out the excessive grip that technology has on our kids. So mark your calendar and make a date.

◆ ◆ ◆

Strategy 40:

Flow

"Flow": Learn to recognize, encourage and respect it.

Flow is that mental state in which a person performing an activity is fully focused and absorbed in the task as hand. Flow has a transcendent quality to it.

Did you ever find yourself immersed in a project—reading an instruction manual, painting a spare room, or doing research on the computer? Suddenly, you're so deeply into the task that you lose track of time and place, and actually begin to find it enjoyable. Work is no longer work. Then, you have entered flow—that state that can carry one along. Effort becomes effortless—it seems that the task at hand is not too hard, not too easy, but just right—(sometimes called the "Goldilocks Effect"). Flow is a strong "Carrot" first identified by creativity guru, Mihaly Csikszentmihalyi in 1990 and since then, strongly tied to learning and creativity.

Adults experience Flow at certain times—but children move in and out of Flow very frequently. Imaginative play, for example is a good example of their Flow. When children are inventing new characters, or creating exciting dialogues, Flow is at work. If they are building a block structure or writing a story, Flow has almost surely arrived. Anytime a child is deeply absorbed in something, chances are, they are in Flow. They are learning and growing—spiraling up to the next level. Serious learning occurs during Flow.

- So watch for it.
- Encourage it.
- Feed it.
- Look for those signs of total absorption, and get out of its way. New learning levels are being accrued and habits of hard work are being cultivated.
- Middle School is a good time to introduce students to the concept of their own Flow. By then, students can recognize and appreciate those special and sacred states.

♦ ♦ ♦

Strategy 41:

"Be Awhile"

"Be awhile." Extend an invitation to "Chill."

I'll never forget the first time I learned the power of the expression, "Be while." While not actually a strategy advocated by the masses, I saw it as a subset of Meditation—a variation of Jon Kabat Zinn's advice to "Be in the moment,"—and decided to include it here.

"Be Awhile," is simple, disarming, and effective in the face of frenzy. This little invitation to "chill" can at times, work wonders, and restore equilibrium—a necessary precursor to work and clear thinking.

"Be Awhile." my friend said softly as he tried to calm our mutual friend.

Our friend was ranting and raving to the two of us about his son "getting the shaft." Another student, a girl, scored higher onan exam, knocking his son out of first place in the running for valedictorian.

"I can't understand how this happened. One lousy test, and it's over. He's been at the top of the class all his life. And now this! So close to the end. He'll never retrieve his position—unless the girl totally blows another course. And I doubt that will happen. It's a tragedy! I don't know whether to kill him, the teacher, or the girl. Just when grades count the most, he drops the ball. All those high hopes. All that scholarship money down the drain!"

The tirade went on and on and on. And for awhile my friend and I sat patiently through the huffing and puffing frenzy.

"My wife and I are beside ourselves," he gasped, slapping himself on the head. "And of course, my son, too, is crushed. Do you think the teacher would let him appeal? Maybe I'll ask to see her grade book. Maybe I'll make an appointment with the principal and demand a complete investigation." He was getting crazier and crazier.

Finally, my friend just leaned over and calmly touched him on the shoulder, and looked the distraught father in the eye. "Be awhile," he said.

"Huh?"

"Be awhile."

That was it. Just, "Be Awhile." That was all it took. Two simple words. And the father suddenly and miraculously calmed down.

"Be awhile, Sam."

And Sam got quiet. He sat back, took a deep breath, and sighed a huge sigh. Then came a few minutes of silence—almost like a forced mini-meditation. Without saying the words, the moment spoke it all: "Relax." "Breathe." "Be calm." "Be in the moment." "Everything will be all right."

"Thanks," said Sam. "I guess I'm over-reacting. I just had to get it off my chest."

In this highly charged, technology-crazed, frenetic, wild, stress-laden, energy blasting era that we all experience at moments, what we occasionally need, is a simple time out. We need time to re-charge, restore, rejuvenate, retrench. Be Awhile. Try it for yourself and your children.

♦ ♦ ♦

Strategy 42:

Meditation

*If ten minutes of meditation can calm him
down and prepare him for learning, why not use it?*

Invoking the "be awhile" strategy is a good one, when those wild and wooly moments erupt. But it's even better to have a planned, structured approach to quiet the mind, restore equilibrium, and pave the way for the unexpected.

Meditation affords such a tact; however, it hasn't always gotten its due.

According to the National Institutes of Health (NIH), meditation is one of the most powerful practices for raising one's cognitive level—and it's been found to have other benefits as well.

For over 6,000 years the practice was a mainstay of many Eastern religions with roots and traditions in Buddhism, Hinduism, Sufism, then later Judaism, and Christianity. But in the West, it has been downplayed. For a long time it was seen as odd—a practice mostly taken up by monks in hillside caves or cloistered nuns, then eventually by hippies. This was definitely not a practice for the mainstream. But then that all changed. Meditation, and its companion practice, "mindfulness," have indeed gone mainstream. Today courses on these topics are taught at major medical centers, universities, and community centers across the nation. The practices are advocated by physicians and health care providers of every ilk. Meditation is for all of us—children included.

Meditation and mindfulness (it's close companion), are defined in various ways: contemplation; emptying the mind of thoughts; concentrating on just one thing at a time to aid mental or spiritual development; relaxation to experience life more fully as it unfolds moment by moment, and more.

In her excellent 2007 tome, *Change Your Mind, Change Your Brain*, science writer, Sharon Begley shares details of an historic 2002 visit by Richard Davidson and other neuroscientists from the University of Wisconsin to an international symposium in Dharamsala, India. At that time Davidson and colleagues invited the Dalai Llama and a group of his friends—Buddhist monks living in the Asian hillsides—to come down from their caves, and visit their lab in America. Here the effects of long term meditation would be studied for the good of science. The invitation was accepted. (It must have been an interesting sight—all those elderly red-robed recluses, prostrate in meditation, with wire hairnets and electronic probes hooked up to their skulls.) At any rate, the research was conducted and the results were definitive: meditation has the ability not only to evoke human compassion, but also to increase mental agility, expand one's capacity for focus and concentration, and even change the physiological structure and size of the brain.

Like Anders Ericsson and his expertise studies before them, this set off many replication and tangential studies which corroborated the findings about the positive and powerful effects of meditation. Refinements still go on today. Together they constitute an important piece of the Great Knowledge Revolution.

In the past decade alone, some of the most exciting research in neuroscience has emerged around the topic of meditation. We now have evidence that meditation can:

Increase attention.

Improve memory retention.

Enhance concentration and ability to focus

Improve problem-solving abilities

Enhance ability to visualize, intuit and express creativity.

Alter the physiological structure of the brain.

Furthermore, there is also proof that in some people, meditation can affect physical and affective processes, such as:

Reducing stress

Aiding physical healing

Managing pain

Alleviating some symptoms of depression and obsessive compulsive disorder

Increasing compassion and kindness

Sensing greater levels of peace, wholeness and well-being

> Children are excellent candidates for meditation. It helps focus their attention, and teaches them self-control. It calms them down.

Almost all of us today are busy—too busy for our own good. Meditation can counter some of that.

Meditation is good for any age—pre-school to senior citizens. It can be as simple or complex as one desires. One can practice meditation or mindfulness meditation for a few minutes or a few hours a day—depending on one's predisposition. It is an ideal antidote for the sensory and technological overload we all experience today. A few minutes a day can clear one's mind, calm one down, and prepare one for a day of rigorous tasks.

Stephan Bodian, author of *"Meditation for Dummies,"* (2010) offers these suggestions for beginners:

1. Begin by sitting comfortably, with your back relatively straight but also relaxed.
2. Take a few deep breaths, relaxing a little on each exhalation.
3. Turn your awareness to the coming and going of your breath. Let your attention focus softly but steadily on your breathing. When your mind wanders off, gently bring it back to your breath.
4. Continue to enjoy your breathing for five or ten minutes or longer. When you're finished, stretch a little, then get up and go about your day.

Many parents used to chuckle and say things like, "Meditation is too Zen for me" or "It's way out there"; however, some have now changed their tunes. One recent reaction was: "Hey, no drugs, no tricks, no gimmicks?… a small investment of time?… only minutes a day to help grow our child's brain, calm him down and prepare him for the day's work? Sure, count us in."

◆ ◆ ◆

Strategy 43:

Show Them the Promised Land

One of a parent's most important jobs is to let your child know that you believe in his future. Your words can be golden. The impression can last forever.

It's been said that the two most important days in your life are:

1. The Day you were born
2. The Day you come to know why.

The first day is easy enough to identify. It's recorded on a piece of paper—a birth certificate. But the second day is more complex. That's the day that one comes to know one's life purpose—the reason you were placed on earth. A few lucky ones just seem to know this from their earliest years. Others experience an "aha" moment. Still others have to work hard—opening and closing a lot of doors along the way; and for a few unlucky ones, that second most important day never comes. And that is truly sad.

We all long for the second day. If one fails, this wreaks havoc with the psyche, and distorts one's life trajectory. Typically, those who don't "come to know why," will drift aimlessly in and out of jobs and careers. And many lives are wasted.

> One of the most important things that parents can do is help their children "come to know why," is to show them the promised land—help them find a vision of their future. Such a vision will drive and sustain them in the future.

Too often this is overlooked by parents. Discouraging remarks tumble out of their mouths: "You're not college material," "You'll never amount to anything." "That's too hard for you," or "You'd better set your sights lower… I doubt that you have what it takes to become that… " Such comments cut deep. The words can resonate and linger in the memory forever. But parents can certainly do their part to encourage their children about their future and help their children "know why" they were put on this earth

Let's review some tips, we've already shared:

- Study the baby from Day One, honing in on interests, talents, proclivities, temperament, and learning styles.

- Respond with opportunities that meet their needs.

- Carry on meaningful conversations throughout the years about their abilities and possible opportunities.

- Dream and visualize with the child about the future. Picture and talk about where all this could lead. Ask them about their own dreams. Where do they want to see themselves?

- Work with them to research some careers that may be suitable to their strengths and interests and to the needs of society. Conjure up some details. In short, show them "the promised land."

Lots of little conversations add up: "I'm so proud that you have such a beautiful voice. We're going to find you a good voice coach, who can bring you along as you grow." Or: "Aren't numbers great? I'm happy you love math and do well in that subject. That makes me proud. Math can really be fun, and there are so many good jobs open to those who work hard at it. Let's look some up some jobs involving math. And let's talk to Mr. Magee down the street. He's an actuary. That's an interesting job."

As they grow, all children wonder: "Who am I?" "Why am I here?" "Where did I come from?" "Where am I going?" "How will I get there?" "How can I serve?" "Why was I put on this earth?" They don't always share this aloud, but parents can encourage these discussions by asking:

What do you like?

What are you good at?

What does the world need?

The answers to these three pivotal questions will provide a platform for serious discussions. You'll help them dream. You can help them plan.

And sometimes it's not the parents who may be the ultimate catalyst. This can come from others, too.

I remember one parent sharing this scenario:

"My son came home one day and told me he finally knew what he wanted to be—a lawyer. I was shocked. He was leaning that way, but had lots of other ideas, too. I asked him how he arrived at that. He told me that the superintendent of schools was passing through the hall in the high school, and stopped him. He said he saw me in the Forensics Finals yesterday, and called me 'outstanding,'—by far, the best debater he had seen in this district. I've been thinking about being a lawyer for a long time, but that did it. That's what I think I'll do.'"

Another father, a musician, talked about a vivid experience he recalled from childhood.

"I had just finished my piano lesson and went outside with the teacher. My mother was waiting in her new car, A BMW.

'Sell this car,' the teacher blurted out.

'Huh?' my mother asked incredulously.

'I said 'Sell this car. You don't need it. What you need is a good piano. More than this car. The car's nice, but you son needs a decent piano more than you need this.'

'What?' my mother asked again in shock.

'That piano inside is a piece of junk. Your son deserves better,' she scolded. 'He's one of the most talented students I've ever seen... maybe the best in all my years. Just sell that car and invest in your son.' Unapologetically she went on and on about my potential. I could hardly believe my ears. That was over thirty years ago, and my ears still burn when I think of it. I was very flattered and it did so much for my confidence. The teacher was right. The piano *was* a piece of junk—decrepit and always out of tune. I think it was a castoff from some local estate sale. But what did I know? I was just a kid.

Well, we didn't sell the car, but at Christmas a Steinway appeared in the living room, and boy did I step up the practice. I was positively giddy and don't know if it was the piano or the vote of confidence from the teacher, but after that, practice was no longer drudgery. She had said I was one of the best, and I kept hearing those words ring in my memory. They still do. From then on, I knew that my career would be in music. And, of course, it has been. And that's brought me great satisfaction."

In their 1986 work, "The Crystallizing Experience: Discovery of an Intellectual Gift," Walters and Gardiner recount single great moments that propelled geniuses toward their destinies. They did not always involve people. Sometimes they involved an encounter with a piece of music or art, but their destiny came to them in a single flash.

One example was Renoir's spellbinding encounter with a piece of 16th century sculpture at the age of twelve. Another was Wagner's "attendance at a performance of Beethoven's opera "Fidelio," after which he wrote a letter to the lead singer dedicating his life to music and then "ran out into the street, quite mad."

One never knows when or if that special moment or crystallizing event will come along. But if and when it does, it helps if a child is prepared, and if the parent has helped shepherd it along.

Now, not all children will be poised for excellence in showy careers—and that's all right. Just remember, all children have some talents—certain proclivities waiting to be honed. It may be caring for others, or a love of numbers, or a love of animals or the environment. It may be cooking or another manual skill. It may be a particular type of service to others. Any interest can be parlayed into a skill and career.

Ounce for ounce and pound for pound, some words hold more weight than others. When you talk about dreams and the future, words hold a lot of weight. They surely get more attention. Did you ever notice how kids perk up when you talk about their future? Hopefully your words will strike a chord because they've grown out of years of observation and prior conversations. When you broach the future, be encouraging. Use the Gaze. Drill down deeply into the child's eyes and offer a gentle touch and kind words. If he appears interested and responsive, go on. Talk about the coming years.

Such moments don't come along every day. They are rare opportunities. Watch for them. Fall upon them when they present themselves, for they are most potent. These are your opportunities that allow you to light a fire and to "Show them the Promised Land."

◆ ◆ ◆

Strategy 44:

Intuition

Gambling aside, never let the children
be afraid to play their hunches.

One of the least recognized aspects of transcendence is the intuitive function. Like religion, this is a topic seldom discussed in schools, though parents bring it up on the side. Some applaud it. Some deny it; others avoid it like the plague. However, I've noticed that parents of highly creative students endorse it and insist that intuition is not used often enough.

Intuition can lead to major breakthroughs—especially when combined with experience and data. It's not uncommon to hear such exclamations as "This neat idea just popped out—just came to me out of the blue," or "Something just told me to go with my gut. I did and it worked out." Intuition, it seems, has given birth to many great ideas.

Renowned astronomer and astrophysicist Carl Sagan, once stated that "mere critical thinking, without creative and intuitive insights, without the search for new patterns, is sterile and doomed. Solving complex problems in changing circumstances requires the activity of both cerebral hemispheres: the path to the future lies through the corpus callosum." (The organ that bridges the two sides.) In other words, the right creative side of the brain when combined with the left or logical side of the brain often produces a superior product.

Albert Einstein respected intuition, too. He once spoke of a simple moment he had while walking down the road with a friend, and suddenly experienced intuition about time and space. We all know where that led.

More recently, futurist Dean Kamen, inventor of the Segway, as well as a wheelchair that can climb stairs, prosthetic limbs and a host of other devices touts intuition frequently. His *First* program (an acronym "For Inspiration and Recognition of Science and Technology) showcases outstanding science and technology projects of young people who have been brave enough to step outside the box. According to Kamen, intuition is essential to anyone who wants to foresee the future and invent new things. That does not, of course, discount the fact that students must also respect what's come before—history and the world of existing knowledge and relevant skill. To intuit fruitfully, they should steep themselves in background facts and processes, just as they let their imaginations fly.

> Ideally, young people should be around adults who respect intuition and see them using their own intuition.

The literature and media are full of examples of great inventors who draw on intuition to create—and sometimes try to explain it— with greater or less success. You may recall the famous *New Yorker* cartoon of two guys looking at a blackboard with an incredibly complicated problem strung out in long formulas. Suddenly one points to a specific area and exclaims, "and then somewhere in here, magic just happens." That was one cartoonist's attempt to explain intuition.

Nowadays, more and more interest seems to be shown in studies of dreams, visualization, imagery, risk-taking, innovation, creativity, intuition and other right brain functions. This is encouraging because researchers increasingly acknowledge these complement our logical left brains and presumably help develop one's holistic potential.

Futurists, in particular, depend on intuition. In fact, intuition is a futurist's stock-in-trade. Today these visionaries are working on projects such Nanobots—(robots built to fight cancer through one's own DNA), anti-aging products, future cities, untold numbers of technology applications and more. In some respects, our survival depends on them. In some large cities, many futurists and inventors now work in "invention labs"—facilities where they work side by side with other kindred souls—inspiring and supporting each other. Some are funded by industry. Others crop up spontaneously. It's an exciting trend and a credit to the culture that has spawned them. One only hopes their influence will continue to spread.

Most likely these pioneers had someone in their past who encouraged them early on—who gave them a green light—the permission to intuit and invent. Along the way, they also learned to endure a few rebuffs and "guffaws," for it seems that most great inventors get ridiculed at times. But they learn to turn a deaf ear, and often get the last laugh.

"Believe in yourself." "Play your hunches," a mentor will say. "Picture the next big idea because someone's got to come up with it. And it may be you."

Parents can help their children by:

- Valuing and trusting their own intuition. Talking aloud about their own instincts at times.

- Listening to themselves and acting on intuitive information when it comes to them.

- Explaining to children how your hunches sometimes play out and pay off.

- Sharing times when they have successfully "gone with their gut," and were pleased with the outcome.

- Limiting their impulsivity. Quieting their minds and focusing their attention to gain a receptive attitude toward one's own intuitions.

- Showing respect for that which is not perceptible—that which cannot be observed or measured.

- Encouraging make-believe and fantasy. Respecting it in others. Telling stories to your younger children and using sound effects and voice changes to enhance the results. Making up plays, finishing open-ended stories, and playing pretending games.

- Joining your children in wholesome videogames that exploit fantasy at times.

- Taking imaginary journeys back in time or to foreign lands. Closing your eyes and talking about the sights, and smells, and characters you meet.

- Watching clouds and other changing images and talking about what they "see."

- Talking about your dreams. Keeping a dream journal.

- Encouraging exploration and a "go for it" mindset from the earliest years.

- Using examples: Explaining what intuition and dreaming meant to Bill Gates, Steve Jobs, Thomas Edison, Henry Ford, the Wright Brothers, Leonardo DaVinci, and many others. Letting them know that they can be part of that line-up, too, if they get comfortable with intuitions and dreams, while delving deeply into content and learning. Remind them it's good to tap your "whole" self.

Lastly, intuition is important because it is related on some level to "consciousness" or the "conscious mind"—a concept that scientists regard as the last great frontier in unlocking the secrets of the brain. Any student wishing to pursue a career in the psychological or biological sciences will surely be well-served if he cultivates a healthy appreciation and learns to exercise his own intuition.

♦ ♦ ♦

Strategy 45:

Energy Sources and Systems

There's something very motivating about trends.
The rising awareness of energy systems, for example,
is one important trend. Keep your kids up to speed
so they can enter the future ahead of the curve.

Keeping up with trends and sharing them with one's children is something that savvy parents have always done, and something many recommend if you want your children to get ahead. Trends can inspire and motivate. Trends can induce transcendence. And trends speak to the future—that beguiling and intriguing entity that draws and fixates their interest. (Instinctively, they must know that the future belong to them.)

Of course, at any moment, there are many trends on the horizon, but one with particular power and promise relates to energy sources and systems, and seems to pepper many conversations with forward-thinking parents. Energy sources and systems are both mysterious and transcendent in nature.

In a 2008 broadcast, Dr. Mehmet Oz told Oprah Winfrey that "energy is the medicine of the future." He highlighted some of its current uses, and implied that this trend will open many more doors, heal many more people, and shed light on our understanding of the intricate interrelationships of our parts to our whole.

> Of course, energy is already "big." It is used to heal, inspire, and even cure many people in greater numbers every day.

For example, electro-shock therapy has come back as a treatment for depression in a much more effective iteration. Also, some disabled persons can now use the energy of their minds to manipulate prostheses and other medical appliances, and going beyond medicine, human brainwaves are also now used to control certain toys and gadgets. Again, too, no one needs to be reminded that the race is on for alternate energy sources to replace fossil fuels before they are depleted. Many energized and innovative citizens have joined that quest with gusto.

People today are also interested in how they can leverage their physical and mental energy. They ask: "What foods and drinks will boost my energy? What environmental conditions help or hurt? How do exercise and weight affect my energy? What thoughts and moods drain me? Why is it that one person's energy field seems to give me a boost, while another's energy drains me? How is it that I can do more work in one hour of a high-energy cycle than in four hours of low energy? How can I increase my overall performance?" It's not unusual for monitoring of one's personal energy levels to go on and on, as does the quest.

One note of caution may be in order, though. The increasing use of "smart pills" (energy-inducing and brain-enhancing drugs, also known as "nootropics") is giving rise to both promise and problems. There is growing evidence that such chemicals, now widely available, can boost attention, memory, concentration, and other abilities related to academic performance. But it is also estimated that 90 percent of certain ones are "off label." That means that a doctor has prescribed them for other than their official purposes—a serious factor for consideration. Researchers constantly debate whether it is safe and fair to allow healthy people to boost their brain function chemically, and the exact ethical and medical implications will probably not be sorted out for some time to come. In the meantime, it behooves parents to stay abreast of the issue.

And then, of course, there's continual interest in the energy exchange that occurs during teaching and learning. We'd all like to know more about this and, in fact, science is studying this, too. More and more of us reflect on the unseen and underappreciated exchanges of energy as parents teach their children.

Recently, I watched a parent bouncing a baby on her knee near a fountain at the mall, and I began to zero in on the energy transfer.

"This little piggy went to market... This little piggy stayed home,." We all know that old familiar tune. She sang it aloud to the delight of both of them—a mutually jovial moment. For some reason, in a flash the definition of "energy" from my old high school physics text passed through my mind. "Energy is the vibrational force around all living cells." And there it was—visible, vibrating human energy playing out in living color at the mall. Baby and mother were giving and receiving energy responsiveness and reciprocity of the highest order, with different types of energy exchanges—each, I concluded aligned to a facet of PACT. There was *Physical* energy—the vibrations and magnetic pulsations given off by the jostling; There was visible *Affective* energy—exuberance, joy, and loving glances. There was *Cognitive* energy—words, a tune, rhythms, rhymes—each presumably new and being soaked up by the baby. And there was *Transcendent* energy—the mutual soaring of spirits—all in the short exchange of a jingle, *"This Little Piggy Went to Market."* I had seen it and played the game numerous times before, but never thought of it this way. Here was energy giving rise to subtle changes beneath the surface: human plasticity at work. I look forward to the day when science helps us better understand how to target our energies to better focus, teach and make the most of those special moments in a holistic way.

Yes, energy in many forms is a very hot topic—rapidly evolving, multi-faceted, and in many ways, transcendent. But of course the definitive playbook has yet to be written. In the meantime, it behooves us to stay tuned.

Transcendence in all forms has the power to inspire and excite and enrich human potential. So embrace its awesome power. And chances are, your children will do the same.

Chapter 8:
Closing

When legendary UCLA coach, John Wooden taught his new players (including Kareem Abdul-Jabbar) how to put on their socks, some balked: "Is he crazy? I didn't come here to learn how to put on my socks. I came here to play competitive college basketball." But Wooden insisted that they pay attention: "One step at a time," he explained. "Little things add up. If you learn the right way to put on your socks, then the socks will not bunch up. And if your socks don't bunch up, you won't get blisters. And if you don't get blisters, you'll be able to run fast. And if you run fast, you'll win more games. And my job is to see that you win games. Have patience. Take a step at a time. And you will see results." And so they did. They learned how to prevent blisters and they had results. Wooden's teams won ten NCAA national championships.

Slow, steady, incremental effort, sustained over time is what moves mountains—in basketball and in effective parenting. If you stay the course, you will eventually see results.

Remember the middle school students from New York City, who were taught that "The mind is a muscle. If you use it, it will grow?" They discovered that mental exercise could change the limits of their brains, just as they already knew steady physical exercise could contour their bodies. Once science had corroborated that, and shown us proof, it was an easy leap to make. Talk to the children about the plasticity of their own minds and bodies. Speak to them, too, about how they can control their own destiny, and how lucky they are to have been born into this age of the Great Knowledge Revolution that has uncovered and explained it. Allow no talk of "bad genes" or limitations. Encourage them to be informed, upbeat and optimistic. And parents should strive to be informed, upbeat and optimistic, themselves, so as to pass those traits on to their offspring.

Inform them that many slow starters pulled ahead through hard work and effort. Those are key. Give them their dreams and encourage them to stretch for lofty goals. But in the end, let them set their own pace. It's okay if your child does not elect to go for the gold—as long as he knows that the choice is his. Each person has his own personal decision to make in this regard.

Parents, too, should only do "what they can do" comfortably. They shouldn't get discouraged by the number of lists in this book. Consider it a handbook or manual, to be perused now, then brought out from time to time through the years, on an "as needs basis."

Remember that there is no right or wrong way to parent. One size does not fit all. Some children will bloom early. Some later. Some will elect not to push themselves. Some will elect to go for the gold. Accept each of your children for who they are, and love them all equally and unconditionally. If you get discouraged at times, remember that most parents raise kids by simply being "good enough," and chances are, you are "good enough" just as you are. If you listen and walk in love, your child will flourish, and you will be a successful parent in every way.

But if you decide you want to raise the bar a little more now, consider some of the suggestions in this book. Assess your child's physical, affective, cognitive, and transcendent profiles. Focus on one goal. If it works, then that is good. Go on to another. But if not, don't give up. Try something different. Then another, and another, and another—as you feel your child is ready—and only if he seems ready, and as you feel ready.

"But my child is almost grown"—or "half grown," some may balk. "It's probably too late." Don't worry. Remember, we are plastic, adaptable beings, responding to inputs and growing new brain cells throughout our lives. We continue to learn as long as we breathe. We have few limitations. We are ever-malleable.

If this still seems overwhelming, remember there are little things that can help a lot:

A hug

A loving glance

A reassuring touch

A warm smile

An animated conversation

Even a single encouraging word

We can easily fit these into our day. They are simple, but they are powerful. And each helps build a brain—slowly and steadily. They can literally change one's physiology for the better.

I commend you, Dear Reader, for picking up this book. That is a good start. Every generation needs to rediscover parenting—to grapple with its complexities and its own situation—and you have begun to do that. It indicates that you are interested in raising the bar for a child—and for the world, which is a very good thing.

Keep this mission close to your heart. It is of prime importance. Even Plato, after a lifetime of study and reflection, came to this final conclusion:

"In the end, there is but one important question: 'Who will teach the children?'"

NOTES:

PREFACE:

McKusick, Victor A. "Eye Color 1." Published on the Online "Mendelian Inheritance in Man" Website, National Center for Biotechnology Information, updated, January 31, 2007.

PART I: THREE KEY BELIEFS: INTRODUCTION

Dweck, Carol. *Self Theories: Their Role in Motivation, Personality and Development,* (Florence, Ky.: Psychology Press, 2000).

Bandura, Albert. *Self Efficacy: The exercise of control,* (New York: Freeman, 1997), p. 604.

CHAPTER ONE: POTENTIAL

Moore, David S. *The Dependent Gene: The Fallacy of "Nature Versus Nurture,"* (New York: Henry Holt and Co., 2003).

Ericsson, K.A. and Chase,W.G., and Faloon, S. "Acquisition of a memory skill," *Science,* 2008, 1980: pp. 1181-82.

Bloom, Benjamin S. (ed.) *Developing Talent in Young People.* (New York: Random House, Inc., 1985).

Ceci, S.J. *On Intelligence: A Bio-ecological Treatise on Intellectual Development.* (Boston, Mass.: Harvard University Press, 1996).

Shenk, David. *The Genius in All of Us,* (New York: Doubleday, 2010), p. 80.

Telis, Gisela, "IQ is Not Fixed in the Teenage Brain," *Science Now,* Oct. 19, 2011.

Jirtle, Randy. "Epigenetics." NOVA. PBS, aired 7/24/07.

Begley, Sharon . *Change Your Mind. Change Your Brain,* (New York: Ballantine Books, 2007).

Pott, Jon. "The Triumph of Genius: Celebrating Mozart." *Books & Culture,* November 2006.

Weisberg, Robert W. "Case Studies of Innovation: Ordinary Thinking, Extraordinary Outcomes." In *The International Handbook on Innovation,* edited by Laris V. Shavinia, Else-vier, 2003.

Brooks, David. "The Heart Grows Smarter," New York Times, Nov. 5, 2012.

CHAPTER TWO: EFFORT

Duckworth, Angela. "Grit: Perseverance and Passion for Long-Term Goals" *Journal of Personality and Social Psychology,* Vol. 92, No. 6, (Wash., DC, 2007).

Wang, Sam, and Aamodt, Sandra, *Welcome to Your Child's Brain*, (New York: Bloomsbury USA Pub., 2011), p. 177, p. 250.

Kochanska, G., Philibert, R.A., and Barry, R.A. "Interplay of genes and early mother-child relationship in the development of self-regulation from toddler to preschool age," *Journal of Child Psychology and Psychiatry 50:1331-38*, (2009).

Sears, William. *Attachment Parenting Book: A Commonsense Guide to Understanding and Nurturing Your Baby*, (Cambridge: Little Brown and Co., 2001).

Chua, Amy. *The Battle Hymn of the Chinese Tiger Mother*, (New York: The Penguin Press, 2011).

Gage, Fred. "An in vivo correlate of exercise-induced neurogenesis in the adult dentate gyrus," *PNAS*, Vol. 104 no. 13 5638-563, March 27, 2007.

Pink, Daniel H. *Drive*, (New York: Riverhead Books, 2009).

Csikszentmihalyi, Mihaly. *Flow: The Psychology of Optimal Experience*, (New York: Harper and Row, 1990).

Caine, Geofrey and Renate. *Making Connections: Teaching and the Human Brain*, (Wheaton, Md.: ASCD, 1991).

Bodrova, Elena and Leong, Deborah J. *Tools of the Mind: The Vygotskian Approach to Early Childhood Education*, (Upper Saddle River, N.J.: Pearson/ Merrill Prentice Hall, 2007).

Dweck, C. S., "The Perils and Promise of Praise," *Ed. Leadership*, Vol 65, No. 2, (Oct., 2007).

Dweck, C. S. *Mindset: The New Psychology of Success*. (New York: Random House, 2006).

Chen, Milton. "Smart Talking: Tell Students to Feed Their Brains," (An e-mail interview of Carol Dweck,) Edutopia, 3/16/07.

Gladwell, Malcolm. *Outliers*. (New York: Little, Brown and Co., 2008).

Lawlis, Frank. *Mending the Broken Bond*. (New York: Viking, 2007).

CHAPTER THREE: BALANCING THE WHOLE CHILD

http://www.ASCD.org. The Association for Supervision and Curriculum Development (ASCD) describes a major strand of their mission—"To Teach" by working with educators and thought leaders worldwide to implement innovative practices focused on the *whole child* and the success of each learner. ASCD has partnered with 38 other organizations in their mission to develop the Whole Child. A recent newsletter stated that "Children's healthy development and its effect on academic achievement is as important today as it was in 1949, (the year the organization was founded.)

http://www.wholechildeducation.org

Siegel, Dan. *The Whole Brain Child*. (New York: Random House, 2012).

CHAPTER FOUR: THE PHYSICAL DOMAIN

Strategy #1—Strong Infant Bonding

Brazelton, T. Berry, and Greenspan, Stanley I. *The Irreducible Needs of Children*, (Cambridge, Mass.: Perseus Publishing, 2000).

Montagu, Ashley. "On Being Human," (A seminar conducted at the Wilmington Country Club on January 10, 1987).

Sears, William. *Attachment Parenting Book: A Commonsense Guide to Understanding and Nurturing Your Baby*, (Boston: Little Brown and Co., 2001).

Strategy #2—The Gaze

Galinsky, Ellen. *Mind in the Making*, (New York: Harper Studio, 2010), p. 118.

Brazelton, T. Berry, and Sparks, Joshua D. *Touchpoints: Birth to Three*. (Cambridge, Mass. : Perseus Books, 2006).

Strategy #3—The Touch

Montagu, Ashley, *Touching: Significance of the Skin*. (New York: McGraw Hill, 1986).

Fields, T, et. al. *Touch*. (Cambridge, Mass.: Bradford Books, MIT Press, 2003).

Brooks, David. *The Social Animal*. (New York: Random House, 2011.)

(A Child Abuse Prevention Program): Child Help: Speak Up. Be Safe: http://www.speakupbesafe.org

Strategy #4—Encourage Exploration

Rendell, Ed. *A Nation of Wusses: How America's Leaders Lost the Guts to Make Us Great*. (Hoboken, N.J.: John Wiley & Sons, 2012).

Medina, John. *Brain Rules for Babies*, (Seattle, Wa.: Pear Press, 2010) p. 103.

Tulley, Gever. *Fifty Dangerous Things You Should Let Your Children Do*. (Montara, Ca.: Tinkering Unlimited Pub., 2009).

Strategy #5—Eye-Hand Coordination

Chua, Amy. *Battle Hymn of the Tiger Mother*, (New York: Penguin Group, 2011).

Medina. John. *Brain Rules for Babies*. (Seattle, Washington, Pear Press, 2010).

Lao-Tzu, (J. Leggee, (trans.) *Tao Te Ching*, Chapter 10B.

Strategy #6—Exercise

May, Linda. Kansas City University of Medicine and Bioscience, *Parade Magazine*, May 31, 2009, p. 22.

Gage, Fred, (ed.) "Exercise training increases size of hippocampus and improves memory," *PNAS (Proceedings of the National Academy of Sciences of the USA,)* January 31, 2011.

Ratey, John. *Spark: The Revolutionary New Science of Exercise and the Brain,* (New York: Little Brown, 2008).

Begley, Sharon. "Can you Build a Better Brain?," *Newsweek and the Daily Beast,* Jan 3, 2011.

NANA (National Alliances for Nutrition and Activity) http://www.schoolwellnesspolicies.org

Strategy #7—Nutrition

Obama, Michele. *American Grown: The Story of the White House Kitchen Garden and Gardens Across America.,* (New York: Crown Pub. Co, 2012).

Seinfeld, Jessica. *Deceptively Delicious.* (New York: Harper Collins, 2008).

Strategy #8—Sleep

Ripley, Amanda. "Teacher, Leave Those Kids Alone," *Time Magazine,* Sept. 25, 2011.

Begley, Sharon. "The Hidden Brain: What Scientists Can Learn From Nothing" *Newsweek, and The Daily Beast* June 7, 2010, p. 24.

Kluger, Jeffrey, "The Creativity of the Sleeping Brain," *Time Magazine,* April 23, 2012, p. 46.

Studies show that lack of sleep has been indicated in: childhood obesity (Cappuccio et al, (2008) and Chen et al. (2008), Krebs et al; in ADHD, (Ronald Chervin and Louise O'Brien Chervon et. al. (2005) poor grades; (Dunner and Wilman, Warner et. Al (2008) and Brackman, et. al (2007); and childhood depression (McKenna, 2007).

MacDonald, Matthew. *Your Brain: The Missing Manual,* (Sebastopol, Ca.: O'Reilly Media, Inc. 2008).

Bronson, Po and Merryman, Ashley. *Nurtureshock,* (New York: The Hachette Book group, 2009).

Barrett, Deidre *The Committee of Sleep* (New York: The Crown Pub., 2001).

Kluger, Jeffrey. "The Creativity of the Sleeping Brain," *Time,* Apr. 23, 2012, p. 44-47.

Strategy #9—Plasticity

Chudler, Eric. University of Washington *Neuroscience for Kids.* (Seattle: University of Washington Press, 2012).

CHAPTER FIVE: THE AFFECTIVE DOMAIN

INTRODUCTION:

Goleman, Daniel. *Emotional Intelligence*, (New York: Bantam Books, 2001).

Brooks, David, *The Social Animal*, (New York, N,Y, Random House 2011).

Strategy #10—Bonding

Tamis-Le Monda, Catherine S., Bornstein, Marc H., and Baumwell, Lisa. "Maternal Responsiveness and Children's Achievement of Language Milestones," *Child Development*, Vol. 72, Issue 3, pp. 748-767. May/June, 2001.

Powell, Alvin. "Decoding Keys to a Healthy Life." *Harvard Gazette*, Feb. 2, 2012.

Montagu, Ashley. *Growing Young*, (New York: McGraw-Hill, 1981).

Strategy #11—Relaxed Alertness

Caine, Geofrey and Renate. *Making Connections: Teaching and the Human Brain*, (Wheaton, Md.: ASCD, 1991).

Strategy #12—Study the Child: Identify His Strengths

Armstrong, Thomas. *Awakening Genius*, (Alexandria, Va.: ASCD Books, 1998).

Strategy #13—Learn Your Child's Interest

Ibid.

Strategy #14—Unconditional Love

Montagu, Ashley. *Growing Young*, (New York: McGraw-Hill, 1981.) p. 133.

The Bible: Corinthians 13:4

Sherr, Lynn. "Oprah Wants You—24/7," *Parade Magazine*, Dec. 26, 2010. P. 7.

Twardosz, S. "Expressing Warmth and Affection to Children." *U.S. Dept. Of Health and Human Services Center for Social and Emotional Foundations of Early Learning.*, August 2005.

Strategy #15—Praise

Dweck, C. S. "The Perils and Promise of Praise," *Ed. Leadership*, Vol 65, No. 2, (Oct., 2007).

Strategy #16—Listen

Faber, Adele. *How to Talk So Kids will Listen*, (New York: Harper-Collins, Inc. 2004).

Senechal, Diana. "Let Us Not Abandon Listening," *Education Week*, August 31, 2011, p. 21.

Strategy #17—Passing on Your Values

Herbert, Todd. "The 'Golden Rule: a List of two Dozen Versions," http://NotAboutReligion.

http:/www.teachkidshow.com/teach-your-child-about-the-golden-rule.

Re: Homework: Boston Public Schools: parentuniversity@bostonpublicschools.org.

Re: Volunteer Jobs for Kids: www.Ask.com

Strategy #18—The Social Landscape

Wilson, E.O. *The Social Conquest of Earth*, (New York, Liveright Pub. Co., 2012).

Christakis, Nicholas. *Time* Dec. 19, 2011, p. 28.

Mogul, Wendy. *The Blessing of a Skinned Knee*, (New York: Scribner), 2008 and Presentation at Congregation Rodelph Shalom, Phila., Pa., April 18, 2012.

Strategy #19—Family Dinners

Doherty, William. *The Intentional Family: Simple Rituals for Strengthening Family Ties*, (New York: Avon Pub. Co, 1997).

ABC News with Diane Sawyer, "Family Dinners Matter for Kids," Sept. 22, 2011.

David, Laurie. *The Family Dinner: Good Ways to Connect with Your Kids One Meal at a Time*, (New York: Grand Central Publishing, 2010).

Strategy#20—Family Meetings

Ibid.

Strategy #21—Goal Setting

Johnson, Vic. *Goal Setting: Thirteen Secrets of World Class Achievers*, (Melrose FL.:No Dream Too Big Publishing Co., 2006).

Feldman, Ruth Duskin. *What Ever Happened to the Whiz Kids?*. (Chicago, IL.: Chicago Review Press, 1982.) Presentation at PAGE Conference, April 28, 1984, King of Prussia, Pa.

Strategy #22—Managing Stress

Seaward, Brian Luke. *Managing Stress: Principles and Strategies for Health and Well-Being*, (Burlington, Mass.: Jones and Bartlett Learning LLC, 2011).

Strategy #22—Self-Discipline & Parental Discipline

Aamodt, Sandra and Want, Sam. *Welcome to Your Child's Brain*, (New York: Bloomsbury USA, 2011), p. 119.

Mogul, Wendy. *The Blessing of a Skinned Knee*, (New York: Scribner, 2010).

Nelson, Jane. *Positive Discipline*. (New York: Three Rivers Press, 2012).

Ginott, Haim. *Between Parent and Child*, (New York: Macmillan, Inc. 1965).

Mogul, Wendy. *The Blessing of a B Minus*, (New York: Scribner, 2012).

CHAPTER SIX: THE COGNITIVE DOMAIN

INTRODUCTION:

Ceci, Rostenblum, deBruyn and Lee. "A Bio-Ecological Model of Intellectual Development," P. xv.

Gardner, Howard, *Intelligence Reframed*, (New York: Basic Books, 2000,) p. 34.

Sternberg, R. J. "Intelligence, Competence, and Expertise." *In Handbook of Competence and Motivation, edited by A.J. Eliot and C.S. Dweck*. (East Sussex, UK: Guilford Publications, 2005).

Eisenberg et Al. *"Nature, Niche, and Nurture," Academic Psychiatry*. Vol. 22. Dec., 1998,) 213-222.

Begley, Sharon. "Can You Build a Better Brain?" *Newsweek, and The Daily Beast*, Jan. 3, 2011.

Begley, Sharon. "Buff Your Brain: 31 Ways to Get Smarter Faster," *Newsweek and the Daily Beast*, Jan. 1, 2012.

Strategy #24—Climate

Biddulph, Steve and Sharon. *Love, Laughter and Parenting*, (New York: Marlowe and Co., 2001).

Sornson, Robt. and Scott, James, (editors,) *Teaching with Joy.*, (Lanham, Md.: Rowman and Littlefield Publishing Group, 2002).

Strategy #25—Making Connections

Spelke, Elizabeth. "The Baby Lab," *The New Yorker*, September 4, 2006.

Galinsky, Ellen. *Mind in the Making*. (New York: Harper Collins Pub., 2010), pp. 157-199.

Strategy #26—Critical Thinking

Brookfield, Stephen. *Teaching for Critical Thinking*. (San Franciso, Ca.: John Wiley & Sons,) 2012.

Parks, Sandra. *Building Thinking Skills*. (various levels) (Seaside, California: The Critical Thinking Company, 2006).

Strategy #27—Problem Solving

Dewey, John. *Essays in Experimental Logic: The Relationship of Thought and its Subject Matter*, (Chicago: U. of Chicago Press, 1916, 75-102) .

Copeland, Matt. *Socratic Circles*, (Portland, Maine: Stenhouse Publishers, 2005).

Gates, Bill and Melinda. "Measures of Effective Teaching Project" at http://www.gates foundation.org.

Strategy #28—Questioning Techniques

Sternberg, Robert J. "Answering Questions and Questioning Answers," *Phi Delta Kappan*, Vol. 76, No. 2, Oct., 1994.

Bloom, B. S., Engelhart, M.D., Furst, E.J., Hill, W.H., and Drathwohl, Dr.R. *Taxonomy of educational objectives: The classification of educational goals; Handbook 1: cognitive domain*, (New York: Longmans, Green, 1956).

Copeland, Matt. *Socratic Circles*. (Portland, Main. Stenhouse Publishers, 2005).

Dewey, John. *Essays in Experimental Logic: The Relationship of Thought and its Subject Matter*. (Chicago: U. of Chicago Press, 1916), 75-102.

Strategy #29—Memory

Begley, Sharon. "Buff Your Brain," *Newsweek*, January 1, 2012.

Kandel, Eric R. *In Search of Memory: The Emergence of a New Science of Mind*. (New York: WW Norton & Co., 2007).

Strategy #30—Creative Thinking

Jobs, Steve. "Life is Just Connecting Things," *Life Hacker*, May 1, 2012.

Diamond, Adele, et al. "Educating the Heart: Creativity and Well-Being and Heart and Mind Education" (A presentation at the Vanguard Peace Summit, Sept. 29, 2009).

Lehrer, Josh. *Imagine: How Creativity Works*, (Boston, Mass.: Houghton Mifflin Harcourt, 2012).

Torrance, Ellis Paul. *Guiding Creative Talent*, (Minneapolis, Mn.: U. of Minnesota Archive, Box Number 1, 1962).

Burstein, Julie and Andersen, Kurt. *Spark: How Creativity Works*, (Public Radio Studio 360, 2011).

Strategy #31—Paying Attention & Self-Control

Begley, Sharon. "Buff Your Brain," *Newsweek and the Daily Beast*, Jan. 1, 2012.

Posner, Michael. *Attention in a Social World*. (Oxford, U.K.: Oxford U. Press, 2012).

Posner, Michael. *Cognitive Neuroscience of Attention: Second Edition*. (New York: Guilford Pub, Inc. 2012).

Bodrova, Elena and Leong, Deborah. *Tools of the Mind*. (Saddle River, N.J.: Prentice Hall Pub., 2006).

smwna.

Strategy #32—Language

Medina. John. *Brain Rules for Babies*. (Seattle, Washington, Pear Press, 2010).

www.goodreads.com

Galinsky, Ellen. *Mind in the Making*, (New York: Harper Collins Pub. Co., 2010), pp. 102-150.

Tamis-LeMonda, C.S., Bornstein, M.H., and Baumwell, C. "Maternal Responsiveness and Children's Achievement of Language Milestones," *Child Development*, 2001 May, June; 72(3) 748-67

Strategy #33—Simple Conversations

(Author's anecdotal experiences)

Strategy #34—Organizational Skills

www.scholastic.com, *Twelve Ways to Help Your Child Develop Organizational Skills*.

Strategy #35—Technology

Kaiser Family Research Foundation: www.kff.org/entmedia/tv.cfm

National Center for Children Exposed to Violence: http:www.nccev.org/violence/media.html.

Strategy #36—Knowing the System

(The website of one's own school district, and/or school is the best source for this.)

CHAPTER SEVEN: THE TRANSCENDENT DOMAIN

INTRODUCTION:

Maslow, Abraham. "A Theory of Human Motivation," *Psychological Review*, 50, pp. 370-396. 1943.

Maslow, A., and Geiger, H., *The Farther Reaches of Human Nature*, (New York: Penguin Bks., 1971).

Strategy #37—Religion.

Fagan, Patrick. "Why Religion Matters Even More: The Impact of Religious Practice on Social Stability," *The Heritage Foundation*, Dec. 18, 2006.

Institute for American Values, "Hardwired to Connect: The Scientific Case for Authoritative Communities," 2002.

Strategy #38—The Arts

Levitin, Daniel. *The World in Six Songs*. (New York: Penguin Group, 2007) p. 15.

McCarthy, K., Ondaatge,E., Brooks, A., and Szanto, A. *A Portrait of the Visual Arts*, (RAND Corporation, 2005).

Strategy #39—Nature

Monaghan, P. and Viereck, E. *Meditation: The Complete Guide*. (New York: Pinnacle Books, 2011).

Kaplan, S. (1995). The restorative benefits of nature: toward an integrative framework. J. *Environ. Psychol.* 15, 169–182. PubMed.

Berman, M.G., et al. (2008). The cognitive benefits of interacting with nature. *Psychol. Sci.* 19, 1207–1212. CrossRef | PubMed.

Strategy #40—Flow

Csikszentmihalyi, Mihaly. Flow: *The Psychology of Optimal Experience*. (New York: Harper and Row, 1990).

Strategy #4—Be Awhile

Kabat-Zinn, Jon. *Coming to Yours Senses*, (New York: Simon and Schuster, 2007).

Strategy #42—Meditation

Begley, Sharon. "Can You Build a Better Brain?" *Newsweek and the Daily Beast*, January 3, 2011.

Begley, S. *Train Your Mind; Change Your Brain*, (New York: Ballantine Books, 2008).

Bodian, S. *Meditation for Dummies*, (Hoboken, N.J. John Wiley, Pub., 2010).

Tang YY, Ma Y, Wang J, Fan Y, Feng S, Lu Q, Yu Q, Sui D, Rothbart MK, Fan M, Posner MI. "Short-term meditation training improves attention and self-regulation," Institute of Neuroinformatics and Laboratory for Body and Mind, Dalian University of Technology, Dalian 116023, China. yiyuan@uoregon.edu.

Monaghan, P. and Viereck, E. *Meditation: The Complete Guide*. (New York: Pinnacle Books, 2011).

Strategy #43—Show Them the Promised Land.

Walters, J. and Gardner, H. *"The Crystallizing Experience: Discovery of an Intellectual Gift."* ERIC ED 254544, 1984.

Strategy #44—Intuition

Sagan, C. *The Dragons of Eden*, (New York: Random House), pp. 190-191.

Kamen, Dean. *First: For Inspiration and Recognition of Science and Technology*, http://www.usfirst.org.

Strategy #45—Energy Systems

Oz, Mehmet. *Dr. Oz Show*, August 31, 2009.

Sparks, Sarah D. "'Smart Pills' Promising, Problematic," *Education Week*, Vol. 32, No. 9, p 1.

CHAPTER EIGHT: CLOSING

Video: *John Wooden Tribute*. PBS 6/7/10. (pbs.org./video #1516714111).

BIBLIOGRAPHY:

Aamodt, Sandra and Wang, Sam. *Welcome to Your Child's Brain*, (New York: Bloomsbury USA, 2011).

Amen, Daniel G. *Magnificent Mind at Any Age.*, (New York: Crown Publishing, Inc., 2008).

Armstrong, Thomas. *Awakening Genius*, (Alexandria, Va.: ASCD Books, 1998).

Bandura, Albert. *Self Efficacy: The exercise of control*, (New York: Freeman, 1997).

Barrett, Deidre. *The Committee of Sleep* (New York: The Crown Pub., 2001).

Begley, Sharon. "Buff Your Brain: 31 Ways to Get Smarter Faster," *Newsweek and The Daily Beast*, Jan. 1, 2012.

Begley, Sharon. "Can You Build a Better Brain?" *Newsweek and The Daily Beast*, Jan. 3, 2011.

Begley, Sharon. *Change Your Mind. Change Your Brain*, (New York: Ballantine Books, 2007).

Begley, Sharon. "The Hidden Brain: What Scientists Can Learn From Nothing" *Newsweek and The Daily Beast* June 7, 2010, p. 24.

Begley, Sharon. "Scans of Monks' Brains Show Meditation Alters Structure and Functioning." *Wall Street Journal*, November 5, 2004, p. B1.

Begley, Sharon. *Train Your Mind; Change Your Brain*, (New York: Ballantine Books, 2008).

Berends, Polly B. *Whole Child/Whole Parent*, (New York, Harper's Magazine Press, 1975).

Berman, M.G., et al. (2008). The cognitive benefits of interacting with nature. *Psychol. Sci.* 19, 1207–1212. CrossRef I PubMed.

Bible, King James Version.

Biddulph, Steve and Sharon. *Love, Laughter and Parenting*, (New York: Marlowe and Co., 2001).

Bloom, B. S. (ed.) *Developing Talent in Young People.* (New York: Random House, Inc., 1985).

Bloom, B. S., Engelhart, M.D., Furst, E.J., Hill, W.H., and Drathwohl, Dr.R. *Taxonomy of educational objectives: The classification of educational goals; Handbook 1: cognitive domain*, (New York: Longmans, Green, 1956).

Bodian, S. *Meditation for Dummies*, (Hoboken, N.J. John Wiley, Pub., 2010).

Bodrova, Elena and Leong, Deborah J. *Tools of the Mind: The Vygotskian Approach to Early Childhood Education*, (Upper Saddle River, N.J.: Pearson/ Merrill Prentice Hall, 2007).

Brazelton, T. Berry, and Greenspan, Stanley I. *The Irreducible Needs of Children*, Cambridge, Mass.: Perseus Publishing, 2000).

Brazelton, T. Berry, and Sparks, Joshua D. *Touchpoints: Birth to Three*. (Cambridge, Mass.: Perseus Books, 2006).

Bronson, Po and Merryman, Ashley. *Nurtureshock*, (New York: The Hachette Book Group, 2009).

Brookfield, Stephen. *Teaching for Critical Thinking*. (San Franciso, Ca.: John Wiley & Sons, 2012).

Brooks, David. "The Heart Grows Smarter," New York Times, Nov. 5, 2012.

Brooks, David. *The Social Animal*. (New York: Random House, 2011).

Bucy, Erik P. and Newhagen, John E. *Media Access: Social and Psychological Dimensions of New Technology Use*, (Mahwah, N.J.: Laurence Erlbaum Associates, 2004).

Burstein, Julie and Andersen, Kurt. *Spark: How Creativity Works*, Public Radio Studio 360, 2011.

Caine, Geofrey and Renate. *Making Connections: Teaching and the Human Brain*, (Wheaton, Md.: ASCD, 1991).

Carr, Nicholas. *The Shallows: What the Internet is Doing to Our Brains*, (New York: W.W. Norton and Co., 2011).

Ceci, S.J. *On Intelligence: A Bio-ecological Treatise on Intellectual Development*. (Boston, Mass.: Harvard University Press, 1996).

Chen, Milton. "Smart Talking: Tell Students to Feed Their Brains," (An e-mail interview of Carol Dweck,) Edutopia, 3/16/07.

Child Help: Speak Up. Be Safe: http://www.speakupbesafe.org.

Christakis, Nicholas. "Putting Social into Science," *Time*, Dec. 19, 2011.

Chua, Amy. *The Battle Hymn of the Chinese Tiger Mother*, (New York: The Penguin Press, 2011).

Chudler, Eric. University of Washington *Neuroscience for Kids*. (Seattle: University of Washington Press. 2012).

Copeland, Matt. *Socratic Circles*. (Portland, Maine: Stenhouse Publishers, 2005).

Csikszentmihalyi, Mihaly. *Flow: The Psychology of Optimal Experience*. (New York: Harper and Row, 1990).

David, Laurie. *The Family Dinner: Good Ways to Connect with Your Kids One Meal at a Time*, (New York: Grand Central Publishing, 2010).

Dewey, John. *Essays in Experimental Logic: The Relationship of Thought and its Subject Matter.* (Chicago: U. of Chicago Press, 1916).

Diamond, Adele, et al. "Educating the Heart: Creativity and Well-Being and Heart and Mind Education" (A presentation at the Vanguard Peace Summit, Sept. 29, 2009.)

Dobson, James. *The Dr. James Dobson Parenting Collection*, (Carol Stream IL,Tyndale House Publishing Co., 2011).

Doherty, William. *The Intentional Family: Simple Rituals for Strengthening Family Ties*, (New York: Avon Pub. Co, 1997).

Druckerman, Pamela. *Bringing Up Bebe*, , (New York: Penguin Press, 2012).

Dweck, C. S. *Mindset: The New Psychology of Success.* (New York: Random House, 2006).

Dweck, C. S. *Self Theories: Their Role in Motivation, Personality and Development.* (Florence, Ky.: Psychology Press, 2000).

Dweck, C. S. "The Perils and Promise of Praise," *Ed. Leadership*, Vol 65, No. 2, (Oct., 2007).

Duckworth, Angela. "Grit: Perseverance and Passion for Long-Term Goals" *Journal of Personality and Social Psychology*, Vol. 92, No. 6, (Wash., DC, 2007).

Eisenberg et Al. *"Nature, Niche, and Nurture," Academic Psychiatry.* Vol. 22. Dec., 1998).

Ericsson, K.A. and Chase,W.G., and Faloon, S. "Acquisition of a memory skill," *Science*, 2008, 1980.

Faber, Adele. *How to Talk So Kids will Listen*, (New York: Harper-Collins, Inc. 2004).

Fagan, Patrick. "Why Religion Matters Even More: The Impact of Religious Practice on Social Stability," *The Heritage Foundation*, Dec. 18, 2006.

Feldman, Ruth Duskin. *What Ever Happened to the Whiz Kid?*, (Chicago, Ill.: Chicago Review Press, 1982.) Presentation at PAGE Conference, April 28, 1984, King of Prussia, Pa.

Fertig, Carol. *Raising a Gifted Child*, (Waco, Texas: Prufrock Press, 2009).

Fields, T, et. al. *Touch.* (Cambridge, Mass.: Bradford Books, MIT Press, 2003).

Friel, John and Friel, Linda. *The Worst Things Good Parents Do.* (Deerfield Beach, Fla.: Health Committee, Inc., 1999).

Gage, Fred. "An in vivo correlate of exercise-induced neurogenesis in the adult dentate gyrus," *PNAS*, Vol. 104 no. 13 5638-5643, March 27, 2007.

Gage, Fred. (ed.) "Exercise training increases size of hippocampus and improves memory," *PNAS (Proceedings of the National Academy of Sciences of the USA,)* January 31, 2011.

Galinsky, Ellen. *Mind in the Making*, (New York: Harper Studio, 2010).

Gardner, Howard. *Intelligence Reframed*, (New York: Basic Books, 2000).

Gates, Bill and Melinda. "Measures of Effective Teaching Project" at http://www.gates foundation.org.

Gladwell, Malcolm. *Outliers*. (New York: Little, Brown and Co., 2008).

Ginott, Haim. *Between Parent and Child*, (New York: Macmillan, Inc. 1965).

Goertzel, Victor, Goertzel, Mildred, Goertzel, Ted, and Hansen, Ariel. *Cradles of Eminence*, (Scottsdale, Arizona: Great Potential Press, 2004).

Goleman, Daniel. *Emotional Intelligence*, (New York: Bantam Books, 2001).

Gopnic, A., Meltzoff, A., Kuhl, P. *The Scientist in the Crib: What Early Learning Tells Us About the Mind*, (NY: Harper Collins, Pub., 1999).

Hightower, Elaine, and Riley, Betsy. *Our Family Meeting Book*, (Minneapolis, MN: Free Spirit Publishing, 2002).

Hyman, Mark. *The UltraMind Solution*, (New York: Scribner, 2009).

Institute for American Values. "Hardwired to Connect: The Scientific Case for Authoritative Communities," 2002.

Jirtle, Randy. "Epigenetics." NOVA. PBS, aired 7/24/07.

Jobs, Steve. "Life is Just Connecting Things," *Life Hacker*, May 1, 2012.

Kabat-Zinn, Jon. *Coming to Yours Senses*, (New York: Simon and Schuster, 2007).

Johnson, Vic. *Goal Setting: Thirteen Secrets of World Class Achievers*, (Melrose Fl.: No Dream Too Big Publishing Co., 2006).

Kandel, Eric R. *In Search of Memory: The Emergence of a New Science of Mind.* (New York: WW Norton & Co., 2007).

Kaplan, S. (1995). "The restorative benefits of nature: toward an integrative framework." Environ. Psychol. 15, 169–182. PubMed.

Killgore, Wm. D.S., "Effects of Sleep Deprivation on Cognition," http://www.ncbl.nlm.nih/pubmed 21075236

Kluger, Jeffrey. "Shhh! Genius at Work," *Time*, Apr. 23, 2012, p. 44-47.

Kochanska, G., Philibert, R.A., and Barry, R.A. "Interplay of genes and early mother-child relationship in the development of self-regulation from toddler to preschool age," *Journal of Child Psychology and Psychiatry* 50:1331-38, (2009).

Kotulak, Ronald. *Inside the Brain*, (Kansas City: Andrews McMeel Publishing, 1996).

Lao-Tzu. (J. Leggee, trans.) *Tao Te Ching*, Chapter 10B.

Lawlis, Frank. *Mending the Broken Bond.* (New York: Viking, 2007).

Lehrer, Josh. *Imagine: How Creativity Works*, (Boston, Mass.: Houghton Mifflin Harcourt, 2012).

Levine, Madeline. *Teach Your Children Well: Parenting for Authentic Success*, (NY: Harper Collins, 2012).

Levitin, Daniel. *The World in Six Songs.* (New York: Penguin Group, 2007).

Louv, David. *Last Child in the Woods: Saving our Children from Nature-Deficit Disorder*, (New York: Workman Publishing Co, 2008).

MacDonald, Matthew. *Your Brain: The Missing Manual*, (Sebastopol, Ca.: O'Reilly Media, Inc. 2008).

Maslow, Abraham. "A Theory of Human Motivation," *Psychological Review*, 50, pp. 370-396. 1943.

Maslow, A., and Geiger, H., *The Farther Reaches of Human Nature,* (New York: Penguin Bks., 1971).

May, Linda. Kansas City University of Medicine and Bioscience, *Parade Magazine*, May 31, 2009, p. 22).

McCarthy, K., Ondaatge,E., Brooks, A., and Szanto, A. A Portrait of the Visual Arts, (RAND Corporation, 2005).

Medina, John. *Brain Rules*, (Seattle, WA: Pear Press, 2008).

Medina, John. *Brain Rules for Babies*, (Seattle, WA: Pear Press, 2010).

Mogul, Wendy. *The Blessing of a Skinned Knee*, (New York: Scribner, 2010).

Mogul, Wendy. *The Blessing of a B Minus*, (New York: Scribner, 2012).

Monaghan, P. and Viereck, E. *Meditation: The Complete Guide.* (New York: Pinnacle Books, 2011).

Montagu, Ashley. *Growing Young*, (New York: McGraw-Hill, 1981).

Montagu, Ashley. *Touching: Significance of the Skin.* (New York: McGraw Hill, 1986).

Nelson, Jane. *Positive Discipline.* (New York: Three Rivers Press, 2012).

Obama, Michele. *American Grown: The Story of the White House Kitchen Garden and Gardens Across America.*, (New York: Crown Pub. Co, 2012).

Olszewski-kubilius, P., Limburg-weber, L., Pfeiffer, St. *Early Gifts: Recognizing and Nurturing Children's Talents*, (Waco, Texas, Prufrock Press, 2003).

Ornish, D., *Love and Survival and the Scientific Brain for the Healing Power of Intimacy.* (New York: Harper and Collins, 1998).

Parks, Sandra. *Building Thinking Skills.* (various levels) (Seaside, California: The Critical Thinking Company, 2006).

Perlmutter, David. *Raise a Smarter Child by Kindergarten.* (New York: Morgan Road Books, 2006).

Pascual-Leone, A., Amed, A., Fregni, F., and Merabet, L.B. "The Plastic Human Brain Cortex," *Annual Review of Neuroscience*: 28, 2005, pp. 377-401.

Pink, Daniel H. *Drive*, (New York: Riverhead Books, 2009).

Posner, Michael. *Attention in a Social World.* (Oxford, U.K.: Oxford U. Press, 2012).

Posner, Michael. *Cognitive Neuroscience of Attention: Second Edition.* (New York: Guilford Pub, Inc. 2012).

Pott, Jon. "The Triumph of Genius: Celebrating Mozart." *Books & Culture*, November 2006.

Powell, Alvin. "Decoding Keys to a Healthy Life." *Harvard Gazette*, Feb. 2, 2012.

Ratey, John. *Spark: The Revolutionary New Science of Exercise and the Brain*, (New York: Little Brown, 2008).

Rendell, Ed. *A Nation of Wusses: How America's Leaders Lost the Guts to Make Us Great.* (Hoboken, N.J.: John Wiley & Sons, 2012).

Reynolds, Gretchen. "How Muscle Workouts May Boost Brainpower," *New York Times*, May 8, 2012.

Ripley, Amanda. "Teacher, Leave Those Kids Alone," *Time Magazine*, Sept. 25, 2011.

Ronney, Karen. Proud Parents' Guide, (Nashville, Ky., Thomas Nelson Pub., 2008).

Sagan, C. *The Dragons of Eden*, (New York: Random House), pp. 190-191.

Schwartz, Jeffrey and Begley, Sharon. *The Mind and the Brain: Neuroplasticity and the Power of Mental Force*, (New York: Harper Collins, 2003).

Sears, William. *Attachment Parenting Book: A Commonsense Guide to Understanding and Nurturing Your Baby*, (Cambridge: Little Brown and Co., 2001).

Seaward, Brian Luke. *Managing Stress: Principles and Strategies for Health and Well-Being*, (Burlington, Mass.: Jones and Bartlett Learning LLC, 2011).

Seinfeld, Jessica. *Deceptively Delicious*. (New York: Harper Collins, 2008).

Senechal, Diana. "Let Us Not Abandon Listening," *Education Week*, August 31, 2011, p. 21.

Shenk, David. *The Genius in All of Us*, (New York, Doubleday, 2010).

Sherr, Lynn. "Oprah Wants You—24/7," *Parade Magazine*, Dec. 26, 2010. P. 7.

Siegel, Dan. *The Whole Brain Child*. (New York: Random House, 2012).

Sobel, David. *Wild Play Parenting Adventures in the Great Outdoors*. (San Francisco: Sierra Club Books, 2011).

Sornson, Robt. and Scott, James (editors). *Teaching with Joy*, (Lanham, Md.: Rowman and Littlefield Publishing Group, 2002).

Sparks, Sarah D. "'Smart Pills' Promising, Problematic," *Education Week*, Vol. 32, No. 9, p 1.

Spelke, Elizabeth. "The Baby Lab," *The New Yorker*, September 4, 2006.

Spock, Benjamin, and Neelman, Robert. *Dr. Spock's Baby and Child Care: 9th edition*, (Cambridge, UK: Cambridge University Press, 2012).

Spock, Benjamin. *Dr. Spock on Parenting*, (Cambridge UK: Cambridge University Press, 2001).

Spock, Benjamin. *Dr. Spock's: "The School Years," The Emotional and Social Development of Children*, (New York: Pocket Books, 2001).

Staff of the Harvard Crimson. Cambridge, Mass. *50 Successful Harvard Application Essays: What Worked for Them Can Help You Get into the College of Your Choice*. Third Edition, (New York: St Martin's Press, 2010).

Sternberg, Robert J. "Answering Questions and Questioning Answers," *Phi Delta Kappan*, Vol. 76, No. 2, Oct., 1994.

Sternberg, Robert J. " Intelligence, Competence, and Expertise." *Handbook of Competence and Motivation*, edited by A.J. Eliot and C.S. Dweck. (New York: Guilford Publications, 2005).

Sternberg, Robert, and Grigorenko, Elena (eds.). *Intelligence, Heredity, and Environment*, (Cambridge, UK: Cambridge U. Press, 1997).

Tamis-Le, Monda., Catherine S., Bornstein, Marc H., and Baumwell, Lisa. "Maternal Responsiveness and Children's Achievement of Language Milestones," *Child Development*, Vol. 72, Issue 3, pp. 748-767. May/June, 2001.

Tang YY, Ma Y, Wang J, Fan Y, Feng S, Lu Q, Yu Q, Sui D, Rothbart MK, Fan M, Posner MI. "Short-term meditation training improves attention and self-regulation," Institute of Neuroinformatics and Laboratory for Body and Mind, Dalian University of Technology, Dalian 116023, China. 2007.

Telis, Gisela. "IQ is Not Fixed in the Teenage Brain," *Science Now*, Oct. 19, 2011.

Torrance, Ellis Paul. *Guiding Creative Talent*, (Minneapolis, Mn.: U. of Minnesota Archive, Box Number 1, 1962).

Tulley, Gever. *Fifty Dangerous Things You Should Let Your Children Do*. (Montara, Ca.: Tinkering Unlimited Pub., 2009).

Twardosz, S. "Expressing Warmth and Affection to Children." *U.S. Dept. Of Health and Human Services Center for Social and Emotional Foundations of Early Learning.*, August 2005.

Walters, J. and Gardiner, H. *"The Crystallizing Experience: Discovery of an Intellectual Gift."* ERIC ED 254544, 1984.

Wang, Sam, and Aamodt, Sandra. *Welcome to Your Child's Brain*, (New York: Bloomsbury USA Pub., 2011).

Webb, J., Gore, J., Amend, E., and DeVries, A. *A Parents' Guide to Gifted Children*. (Tucson, AZ: Great Potential Press, 2007).

Weisberg, Robert W. "Case Studies of Innovation: Ordinary Thinking, Extraordinary Outcomes." In *The International Handbook on Innovation*, edited by Laris V. Shavinia, Else-vier, 2003.

Will, George F. "Lost in Electronica," *Newsweek*, August 23 & 30, 2010, pp. 28-29.

Wilson, E.O. *The Social Conquest of Earth*, (New York, Liveright Pub. Co., 2012).

Winnicott, D.W. "Transitional objects and transitional phenomena," *International Journal of Psychoanalysis*, 34:89-97, (Hoboken, NJ., 1953).

Zarin, Jill, Wexler, Lisa, and Kamen, Gloria. *Secrets of a Jewish Mother*. (New York: Penguin Group, 2010).

HELPFUL LINKS:

GENERAL PARENTING:

U.S. Department of Education, www.ed.gov/parent/landing.jhtml
National Education Association, NEA, www.nea.org
National Coalition for Parent Involvement in Education (NCPIE),
www.ncpie.org
Zero to Three, www.Zerotothree.org
The Family Education Network, www.familyeducation.com
The National Parenting Center, www.tnpc.com
Parent Center, www.parentcenter.com
Parenting.com, www.Parenting.org
Parenting Resources for the 21st Century, www.parentingresources.ncjrs.org
Parent Teacher Association (PTA), www./pta.org
National Education Association, www.Nea.org
Kaiser Family Research Foundation: www.kff.org/entmedia/tv.cfm
American Academy of Pediatrics Ages and Stages,
www.aap.org/healthtopics/stages.cfm
Dr. Spock, www.drspock.com
Alliance for Childhood, www.Allianceforchildhood.net
Foundations for Early Learning, www.Earlylearning.org
National Association for the Education of Young Children (NAE),
www.naeyc.org

PARENTING FOR HIGH POTENTIAL

National Assn. for Gifted Children, www.nagc.org
Hoagies Gifted Education Page, www.hoagiesgifted.org
Gifted Education Communicator, http://www.cagifted.org,
www.luminosity.com/blog/brain-training-for-kids, www.brainology.us

PLASTICITY and BRAIN SCIENCES

Institute for Learning and Brain Sciences, www.ilabs.washington.edu
National Center for Biotechnology Information, www.pubmed.gov

EFFORT:

www.sowhatireallymeans.com

WHOLE CHILD EDUCATION:

http://www.wholechildeducation.org

THE PHYSICAL DOMAIN:

American Academy of Pediatrics, www.aap.org/
American Academy of Pediatrics Ages and Stages,
www.aap.org/healthtopics/stages.cfm
Society for Adolescent Medicine
www.adolescenthealth.org

Exercise:
www.nim.nih.gov/medicineplus/exercise/children.html

Nutrition:
NANA (National Alliances for Nutrition and Activity),
http://www.schoolwellnesspolicies.org
www.choosemyplate.gov

Sleep:
www.webmd.com/parenting/guide/sleep-children
www.cdc.gov/features/sleep

THE AFFECTIVE DOMAIN:

Committee for Children/social skills training, www.Cfchildren.org
Personal Safety: http://www.speakupbesafe.org
Homework Guidelines, parentuniversity@bostonpublicschools.org
Empathy, www.Rootsofempathy.org,
www.teachkidshow.com/teach-your-child-about-the-golden-rule
Children and Adults with Attention Deficit/Hyperactivity Disorder:
(CHADD), www.chadd.org
American Academy of Child and Adolescent Psychiatry, www.aacap.org
Volunteer Jobs for Kids: www.Ask.com
Federation of Families for Children's Mental Health, www.ffcmh.org

THE COGNITIVE DOMAIN

Literacy:
www.Goodreads.org

Math and Science:
American Library Association, www.ala.org
Association for Women in Science, www.Awis.org
Study Guides and Strategies, www.studygs.net,
www.ucc.vt.edu/stdysk/stdyhlp.html
Expanding Your Horizons in Science and Mathematics,
www.Expandingyourhorizons.org
Kahn Academy Academic Courses, www.Kahnacademy.org
www.bedtimemath.org

Gifted:
Johns Hopkins University Center for Talented Youth. www.Cty.jhu.edu
Imagine Magazine, http://cty.jhu.edu/imagine

Internet Safety:
www.Webwise.org
www.Wiredsafety.org
www.Safekids.com
www.BlogSafety.org
www.GetNetWise.org
Kaiser Family Research Foundation, www.kff.org/entmedia/tv.cfm
National Center for Children Exposed to Violence:
www.nccev.org/violence/media

THE TRANSCENDENT DOMAIN

Nature:
www.natureforkids.net

The Arts:
www.nea.gov/pub/imagine.pdf

Flow:
www.primarygames.com/puzzles/strategy/letflow,
www.flowcircuskids.com

Meditation:
www.children.meditation.org.au/
www.trymentalworkout.com
Meditation and Brain Plasticity., yiyuan@uoregon.edu

ABOUT THE AUTHOR

Dr. Marjorie DelBello is an educator with over forty years experience in the field. She holds a B.S. in Ed. from Temple University, a M.S. in Ed. from The University of Pennsylania, and an Ed.D. from Temple University in educational leadership. She has served as a classroom teacher, teacher of the gifted, principal, supervisor, adjunct university professor of gifted studies, and Assistant Superintendent of Schools in the Garnet Valley School District in Glen Mills,  Pennsylvania. Dr. DelBello has also served as a consultant to *Newsweek* Magazine, and is the recipient of numerous grants and awards, including finalist, Pennsylvania Gifted Teacher of the Year (1989), "Peacemaker of the Year" (2003), (Center for Resolutions, Delaware County, Pennsylvania); and Educator of the Year, SAP, Inc. (2001). She has served as a consultant in a number of capacities, including coordinator of educational exchanges between American and Chinese schools. Dr. DelBello is the parent of two children, and grandparent of two. She resides in Philadelphia, Pennsylvania, with her husband, James, and can be contacted at *delbelm@gmail.com*.

30819230R00154

Made in the USA
Lexington, KY
18 March 2014